Praise for Major Gifts Unwrapped

C000048745

"The roles of the social entrepreneur becoming ever more critical to the m society. This book provides some practical advice for social entrepreneurs wanting to confront the lack of understanding that exists between them. If you're serious about finding a win-win, it's for you"
Andrew Edmiston, Founder of Imagine the Day, Managing Director of IM Group Limited

"Great to see one of our longstanding members contributing to the sharing of ideas around excellent fundraising – which is what the Institute is all about"
Peter Lewis, Chief Executive, Institute of Fundraising, UK

"Ruth's book is packed with powerful principles, ideas and case studies for raising millions for your charity. If you are a major donor fund raiser, whether seasoned with experience or starting out, you need to read this book!"
Matt Bird, Founder of Cinnamon Network International

"Ruth nails every possible situation you will face in major gifts in this amazing, helpful and professional book. Read every word and then be sure and follow each of her principles and you will find success in major gifts"
Richard Perry, Founding Partner, Veritus Group, Co-author Passionate Giving Blog

"Ruth is an exceptional fundraiser and fundraising consultant. I have seen first-hand how following her practical approach to major gift fundraising delivers transformational results for charities and life enhancing experiences for donors. I highly recommend this insightful yet practical book"
Graeme Newton, Director of Fundraising, World Vision UK

i

"Arts, cultural and heritage fundraising has led the way in combining major gifts with excellent stewardship and engagement of whole families. Many other sectors of fundraising can learn from our experience, and I am delighted that Ruth Irwin has so effectively dealt with both the tools of the trade as well as the tradecraft in a book that crosses all sectors. The cultural sector has been fighting to overcome severe budget cuts, and a mass take up of major gift excellence is one way to address our future sustainably. Ruth should be applauded for the impact she will undoubtedly have in the world of arts fundraising"
Martin Kaufman, Chair, Institute of Fundraising Cultural Sector Network; Principal, Martin Kaufman Philanthropy

"Ruth is practical, passionate and dedicated to major gift fundraising. She wants to make the world a better place and knows what she is saying, as it is all grounded in so much depth of expertise and personal knowledge. Having worked alongside Ruth for a number of years, I can attest that all the principles in this book have been proven and tested resulting in great success for the fundraising executive and the organisation. This book is packed with so much wisdom and insight, it is a must for everyone who loves fundraising"
Folashade Komolafe MBE DL, Chairman Indisys Business Solutions, Strategic Consultant Mazars, Founder Fresh Inspiration, Board Chair Milton Keynes Foodbank, Vice President British Red Cross

"Ruth's book fills a big gap in the market - a really practical 'how to' approach for major giving. It will be equally invaluable to those just starting a major gift programme as well as those who want to review how well their existing programme is working. A 'five star' recommendation from me"
Andrew Barton, Independent Consultant and former Fundraising Director at Oxfam, Great Britain

"We have been working with Ruth to develop a major gift programme and have benefitted hugely from her wisdom, knowledge and experience in this field. The integrity of her approach to major gift philanthropy greatly resonates with us here at BRF. Her attention to detail and the mentoring she has provided to our new team are second to none. We would recommend her without hesitation"
Richard Fisher, Chief Executive, The Bible Reading Fellowship

"I would highly recommend Ruth's book to anyone, whether you are starting out in your first role as a major donor executive or whether you manage a team of more advanced fundraisers. Ruth's methodology and experience will give you a way to approach prospecting and managing your workload which can only lead to success"
Mary Smith, Associate Director of Leadership Giving, Habitat for Humanity International

"We did not have a major donor programme at United Christian Broadcasters. Ruth skilfully helped UCB set up the programme, prepare job descriptions, train staff and instigated all the processes needed. I am certain readers of this much-needed book will experience, as we did, Ruth's guidance, support, energy and enthusiasm for their major donor programme"
Sheron Ferguson, Director of Communications, United Christian Broadcasters

"This book is a gold mine – literally. There is nothing Ruth does not know about major donor fundraising. Ruth is a brilliant strategist and planner, and extremely knowledgeable in every aspect of major donor fundraising. The work she did for us developing the major donor programme and processes from scratch has proved sustainable and invaluable for the League. I recommend this book to any charity looking for expert advice on major donor fundraising"
Philippa King, Chief Executive, League Against Cruel Sports

"This book is full of wonderful information and needs to be read by anyone dealing with major donors. The principles Ruth champions are imperative and should be followed in order to maximise the funds charities need to raise"
Kay Honner, Major Partnerships Manager, Helen & Douglas House, Hospice Care for Children and Young Adults, Oxford

"Are you a hunter or a nurturer when it comes to major gifts? And what is a major gift anyway? This book is full of practical advice and examples that will help you raise the bar, in more senses than one. 'Major Gifts Unwrapped' is like having your own fundraising consultant delivered to your door – gift wrapped!"
David Saint, Chairman, Action Planning

"This book sets out, with great clarity, the key principles any major donor fundraiser should adopt. Ruth's approach comes from experience at the 'coal-face' – her examples demonstrate what works!"
Jim Gilbourne, Chief Executive, Mission Housing

"Ruth skilfully and patiently taught me the A – Z of major donor fundraising and shared her wealth of knowledge and personal experiences that brought to life my learning. Ruth has an outstanding ability to bring out the best in everyone she mentors. This book will challenge you to achieve things you thought were impossible"
Saramine Mukute, Senior Philanthropy Executive, World Vision Philanthropy Team

Coming soon:

Major Gifts Unwrapped – Book Two

*49 Principles for the **Accomplished** Major Donor Fundraiser*

Book Two includes the following:
- Characteristics of an effective major donor executive
- How to effectively engage your leadership
- Structuring the team
- How mid value and major gift programmes work together
- Use of capital campaigns
- Understanding a philanthropist's motivations
- Levels of engagement before the 'ask'
- Writing an effective 'ask' proposal
- How to ask for a gift
- Using multi-year 'asks'
- Levels of stewardship after the 'ask'
- Donor visits to your office - 'Red Carpet Days'
- Importance of donor memories
- Common problems and how to overcome them

BOOK ONE

MAJOR GIFTS UNWRAPPED

39 PRINCIPLES FOR THE SUCCESSFUL MAJOR DONOR FUNDRAISER

RUTH IRWIN

BOOK ONE
MAJOR GIFTS UNWRAPPED
39 PRINCIPLES FOR THE SUCCESSFUL MAJOR DONOR FUNDRAISER

Published in the United Kingdom by
Ruth Irwin
Great Brickhill, MILTON KEYNES
MK17 9AS, United Kingdom

www.ascentphilanthropy.co.uk

Cover design by Book Beaver

Printed in the United Kingdom

This publication is designed to provide accurate and authoritative information for Fundraising Executives. It is sold under the express understanding that any decisions or actions you take as a result of reading this book must be based on your own judgment and will be at your sole risk. The author will not be held responsible for the consequences of any actions and/or decisions taken as a result of any information given or recommendations made.

This book is published with British spellings

For example, the word 'practice' is a noun and 'practise' is the verb in British spelling

ISBN-10: 1999906209
ISBN-13: 978-1999906207

To my husband Simon with love and gratitude
for his constant love and support

CONTENTS

Foreword

I was first introduced to major donor fundraising over 30 years ago. I loved it from the beginning and understood clearly in those early days that there are philanthropists who are looking to give money away to great causes, fulfilling their values to contribute to society and there are visionary non-profits looking to fund their creative dreams to support beneficiaries. I have never viewed major donor fundraising as trying to coerce someone to give their money away, it is rather a bringing together of those who have wealth with non-profit specialists who can advise on how best to spend it, whether a charity to help the vulnerable, an art gallery or even a university. It is a mutual partnership.

It is personally beneficial to the funder because there is great joy in giving. One wealthy individual said to an executive I was coaching 'I have never given a gift this size before (£35,000) and it has been an amazing experience'. I have always based my coaching work with executives on the value of the joy of giving. It is transformational. In most cases the giver will experience long-lasting, deep satisfaction in seeing all their money has achieved. This is true philanthropy.

Your part as the fundraiser is to find the right project match, provide the vision of what can be achieved and then conscientiously feed back to the funder the difference they have made. Your enthusiasm and belief in your work is infectious to those who want to make a difference in the world. The interesting part for you, the major gift executive, is that philanthropists are individuals and no two are the same. What is appropriate for one is far from appropriate for another!

I am particularly grateful to Richard Perry, Founder of Veritus Group, author of the Passionate Giving blog, whom I worked with twelve years ago and who heavily influenced my thinking and methodology for the programme, adding to my previous 20 years working in this field.

What I have written in this book is my first hand experience of both training new major gift executives, improving performance with major gift teams and, at various times in my career, performing the role myself. I have tried to identify the biggest issues that I have come across in the programme and write down everything I have learned, sharing my first-hand knowledge of what works. My aim is to help you build a successful programme that will increase your income year on year.

I would also like to thank friend and colleague, Mary Smith, who painstakingly went through this book adding her comments and corrections which grounded me and was really helpful.

Finally, my enormous thanks to Fola Komolafe, who worked with me as a consultant with a number of clients. Fola is a master in organisational culture and how to develop a culture of philanthropy within an organisation to become 'business as usual'. I learned so much from Fola in the years we worked together.

On a practical note the major gift programme, in this book, refers to *individuals* giving personal, philanthropic gifts rather than gifts from corporate trusts, businesses or government. A philanthropist may choose to give this through a personal trust or even their company but at the end of the day it is a personal gift from an individual, a significant gift because an individual or couple like your cause and want to support your work.

In this book I have referred to donors who have not yet given a 'significant' gift, but may have given a smaller donation, as 'prospective major donors' which seems friendlier than referring to them as prospects. They are mostly previous donors on the database who have not yet risen to the height of giving a gift over £10,000.

I also refer quite often to a 'caseload'. This refers to donors who have been qualified by the major gift executive. In other words, you have spoken to them, met them and they are willing to engage further with you and your organisation. Many donors you speak to may not want to continue the relationship. I use the term 'caseload' to delineate those who are happy to journey further with you in a philanthropic relationship.

You won't find much information in this book about peer-to-peer fundraising as, in my view, this is full of difficulties. It works extremely well within capital campaigns where one-off gifts (albeit committed over 3 – 5 years) are the main fundraising focus for the development board, however for setting up a new major gift programme, the relationship should be built over many months with a variety of the organisation's staff rather than passing the relationship and 'ask' over to be managed by someone more remote from your organisation. Introductions, yes of course, however it is important to manage the relationship yourself with the assistance of leadership and your trustees. I have written more about this in *Major Gifts Unwrapped Book Two.*

If you live and work in the United Kingdom or any EU country, it is important to be lawfully compliant with the General Data Protection Regulation (GDPR). In Principle 9 I have included a list of those who can assist you with ensuring you are lawful. Consultant Andrew Barton, who has extensive fundraising experience having worked at senior and Board level at Oxfam and World Vision, has written a variety of practical ways you can ensure that your organisation is compliant with GDPR regulations. These regulations also apply for any overseas organisation looking to approach a UK or EU philanthropist.

I hope you find this book to be a practical 'how to do it' book. I honestly think it is one of the most difficult programmes to get right. Over the years I have attended major donor seminars and noticed that much of what is presented is theory. It is very easy to grasp the theory of major donor work but it is enormously difficult to practise it. I have therefore wanted to focus on the detail of practice. I hope there is lots of information for you to consume in this book and that you can dip in and out of it as you successfully walk your journey in the major gift field. There are certain ingredients that bring success and these I want to share with you within these pages.

Who is this book for?

This book is aimed at coaching major donor fundraisers or senior leadership of an organisation who are seeking to secure £10,000+ gifts in one year from each donor on their qualified caseload whether cumulative or in one gift. The programme described is for any size organisation or charity.

It is therefore aimed at fundraisers of both small and large nonprofits. Having said that, Mary Smith, has pointed out it is also dependent on whether an organisation can actually put together the funding needs for a suitable, costed proposal for £10,000 or more ready for a major donor to fund! It isn't always easy being able to cost your expenditure into £10,000+ attractive chunks that philanthropists may choose to fund.

This book is also for those fundraisers who may feel tempted to 'wing it'. Major gift programmes can often be quite random and sometimes dependent on the strength of the person managing the relationships. If you have a charismatic personality and tend to rely on that, then the processes in this book will help ground you to be successful over the longer term.

Finally this book is intended for a global readership. The principles for philanthropy and setting up a major gift programme within your non-profit apply to any country in the world.

My hope is that whether you are a trustee, chief executive, manager or fundraising executive you can read and apply these principles for success.

I am interested in your experiences and am contactable in the following ways:

Web: www.ascentphilanthropy.com

Email: ruth@ascentphilanthropy.co.uk

Twitter: @ruthascent

It is my greatest hope that you have great success in your major donor programme. If I have played a part in increasing your organisational income from major gifts and in turn your work is transforming more lives for good, I am delighted!

Thank you for reading this book and please leave a review.

Ruth

principle _____ 1

The successful executive plans for no income in the first year

I started with this principle first because, in my experience, seeking quick income from a major gift programme erodes the success of the programme faster than any other factor. It takes a minimum of one year to set up the programme and often nearer to three years. There are many processes that need to be put in place to ensure the programme's success as described further in this book.

To be successful you need to accept that there will be very little income received from the major gift programme in the first year. If you declare this at the very beginning, no-one is disappointed. It is all too easy to give up after the first year when not much income has been raised. A trustee or senior staff member might feel tempted to say 'well that didn't work'. You might feel tempted to leave or worse still the chief executive might not renew your contract.

Just having wealthy names on your database is not enough. Each needs to be contacted one by one to explore if there is synergy and interest in your work. As well as all the internal processes that need to be set up, it takes time for prospective major donors to get to know you and for you to build the relationship sufficiently to ensure there is a match and to qualify them on to your managed caseload. Also, new processes need to be set in place throughout the organisation. It takes time to establish a culture of philanthropy where all staff recognise their role in the major gift process.

I would like to give credit here to Richard Perry of Veritus Group who first introduced me to the concept of 'qualifying' individuals in a major gift programme. It has been used for decades in a business setting however Veritus originated this strategy in a donor context.

As an executive, you should not feel pressured to ask donors to give too soon just to keep your trustees appeased, especially in year one. You need to take time to build trust in the relationships long before asking for a £10,000+ gift and this can often take 12 – 18 months. Every prospective major donor has an individual journey. You need to gauge where the person is on that journey and ask for a gift when you are both ready. It requires great skill. You certainly should not feel pressured to ask too soon to reach an unrealistic financial target.

Picture the Scene.......

An executive felt the pressure from leadership to 'get the money in' and asked a wealthy business man for £50,000 far too early in the relationship. He in fact gave £1,000, however he was keen to continue the relationship and was interested in the work.

He certainly hadn't said 'this is all I am going to give!' He just wasn't ready to give more and still had questions that needed to be answered.

The income will be low in the first year because, for example, a potential £100,000 donor may only want to give £2,000 as he or she is still testing out the water and thinking through whether they like you, whether your cause matches their goals, how you thank them (even for their small gift!), what you are offering, how they get on with your chief executive, whether they believe the organisation can deliver what it says it will and they may potentially have heavy financial commitments to other causes. It is natural for cautious investment at the early stage.

To achieve an income of 1:2 (spend £1 for £2 raised) or 1:3 in the first year is not impossible if you have a database of current donors, however it will normally include donors who gave last year or the previous year and who are due to give again. It is not always the case that there are previous substantial givers, therefore be prepared to accept a fundraising ratio of 1:0 or 1:1. However this can rise quickly in year two and has the potential to reach 1:5 by year three. Here are specific examples of where this happened:

Organisation 1

One full-time executive was raising just under £400,000. Senior leadership decided to invest in the major gift programme. A further three full-time major gift executives were added, one full-time administrator and one full-time prospect researcher. By year three, the annual income from this programme had risen to £2.25 million.

Organisation 2

One full-time trusts' officer was raising approximately £175,000 per annum. Senior leadership invested in a new major gift programme. The trusts' officer switched her role to a major gift executive and two further full-time major gift executives were recruited together with a full-time administrator. By year three, income from the programme had risen to almost £900,000.

Both organisations could have given up at the end of year one as very little income was raised, but by year three, the income from wealthy individuals was flowing and giving a healthy return on investment.

To illustrate more practically why it is rare to receive much income in the first year of the programme, the chart below shows a typical prospecting phase for a new major gift programme.

Year 1

Donors	Jan	Feb	Mar	Apr	May	Jun	Jul	Aug	Sep	Oct	Nov	Dec	Total
Contacted			3	8	6	6	6	3	6	4	4		46
Unqualified			1	3	2	2	3	1	2	2	2	2	20
Cumulative number			2	7	11	15	18	20	24	26	28	26	26
Qualified				1	1	3	3		3	3	3		16
Asked							2		2	2	2		8

Key:
Contacted = the number of donors the executive actually speaks to

or makes contact with, for example, 3 donors were contacted in March, 1 was not interested and unqualified, 2 progressed to the next stage

Unqualified = the number of donors who are not interested in pursuing the relationship or who the executive deems should not be pursued

Cumulative = the number of donors the executive is in dialogue with and looking to qualify on to their caseload

Qualified = the number of individuals who are keen to continue the relationship and hear more about the organisation; they become the executive's 'qualified' caseload

Asked = the number of donors who have been asked for a substantial gift and, only in year one, if they have previously given

The first two months of employment as a major gift executive are normally taken up with a thorough induction. By month three when the executive is ready to approach donors, it is likely that only 3 people are approached initially as the executive gains confidence. This assumes that *many more* attempts have been made but actual contact has only been achieved with 3.

In the following two months maybe only 6 - 8 are contacted in each month. It is a slow build depending on how warm each donor is to the organisation. It is quite common that only 1 in 3 of these might mature into a qualified significant donor because it is likely that 2 out of 3 will not be interested or may be fully committed to other charitable organisations.

After month five of prospecting, up to 30 individuals potentially have been contacted, and very few have been qualified as it often takes over three months of relationship building to qualify even one donor. In conclusion, expect no income for the first eight months unless the individuals contacted have given previous major gifts and may be ready to give again.

After twelve months, out of 46 contacted, only a maximum of 16 are likely to have been qualified on to the executive's caseload, approximately one-third, although relationships are still being maintained with 26 donors each month (numbers in bold). It is a very intensive time. Some can be asked for a gift in year one but most will be asked in year two. Only those qualified in April to July on the chart will perhaps give in year one to December. Even then it may be too soon. It depends on how warm they are to the organisation, when they last gave and whether they have given before.

As you can see, the process is highly time consuming, may involve a number of steps and has to be done on an individual basis. Endless phone calls are made to even make contact with one donor.

You should not lose heart as this very quickly progresses in year two and year three as your relationships deepen. Further donors may be found on your database as described in more detail in Principle 9. A further 12 donors qualified in year two brings the total to 30 donors with a likely income of £200,000+. Often this can be up to £300,000 if a further 10 donors are qualified in year three. In which case, a competent major gift executive will have reached a qualified caseload of 40 individuals or couples giving between them over £500,000.

If you have many high net worth individuals on your database then employing two major gift executives with one administrator at this first stage is very effective. They can train together, support each other and give the programme momentum. Your programme will grow faster and you will reach a 1:5 or 1:6 fundraising ratio much more quickly.

In summary, for a £100,000 investment, you might expect to break even (at best) in the first year, raise £250,000 - £300,000 in the second year and perhaps £400,000 - £500,000 in the third year. If the government's tax refund for donors, called gift aid in the UK, is included this £ figure would be even higher. However if you have a high number of wealthy individuals on your database who have a strong commitment to the cause it is possible to achieve higher than this. In the longer term, it is quite feasible for an executive to bring in over £500,000 income per year and even up to £1 million from their qualified caseload of donors.

The return on investment will continue to increase if the processes of the programme are set up correctly and closely adhered to. The programme is a long term commitment and needs to be considered in this way. It is definitely not a programme for short term gain. There are many factors that contribute to success and these need to be considered in a risk assessment before investing in the programme, often referred to as an organisational readiness study.

The successful executive facilitates an organisational readiness study

There are many reasons why setting up the major gift programme does not gain traction in the early stages. It is good practice to ask a knowledgeable external executive or consultant to do a simple organisational readiness feasibility study for you. The study looks at potential risks for your organisation. It is possible for you to conduct this yourself but just bear in mind that you may bring prejudice to the study and your leadership may not take as much note of the findings if the report is written internally.

Undertaking a risk assessment informs and educates the leadership about the programme. It helps them to understand how much investment is needed, how long it takes to see financial results, how much time is required from leadership and department heads including finance, supporter care, communications and the programme teams.

It can spell out how it will impact the organisation time wise and what commitment is involved and from whom. It will give the best chance for strong foundations to be set in place if everyone understands what is required. It will allow the programme to eventually become 'business as usual' throughout the whole organisation.

The aim is always to build on the success of current activity and to offer some concrete recommendations for instigating the new programme. The aim is for the programme to be successful and grow year on year. It is a good time to check that all staff are supportive of this new programme and understand the need to build relationships with wealthy donors. Identifying the weak areas before the programme is started will build confidence.

Organisational readiness for the programme needs to be assessed. It is very similar to undertaking a risk assessment. What are the strengths? What are the chances for success? Or even failure?

When I perform an organisational readiness study, I look at current performance under a number of different headings using a series of questions to a cross section of staff. Looking at strengths and weaknesses within these headings is very helpful and begins to give focus as to how many tasks need to be achieved and the appropriate staffing required to achieve a successful result. I have listed out some key questions below.

Reasons for the programme
What is the background for wanting to increase funding?
Why is it important to develop this programme? Is everyone supportive?
Why is the timing good now? How urgent is the need?
Is the investment sufficient enough to build a successful programme?
What is unique about the organisation? What are its key selling points?
What will be the philosophy for the major gift programme?
Are all staff in favour of the new programme?
Is there unity on where the new income will be allocated?

Resourcing the team
What is the structure of the current fundraising team?
Is the team sufficiently resourced?
Who does what? How will this change?
How much will need to be invested? In which roles?
Where are the gaps?
Will the team be supported when the programme is implemented?

Current major donors
What major donors are there currently? Are they being looked after? How will this change?
Are there sufficient numbers of wealthy individuals on the database?

How are donors currently thanked? What needs to be added to these processes?

How are plans currently tracked for each major donor?

Do the major donors keep giving?

What happens to lapsed mid and major donors?

Is there sufficient project information for major donors?

What is currently sent to them?

How are current major donors engaging with staff?

How should major donors be engaged in the future?

Are volunteer peer to peer fundraisers used?

Is there a mid value programme? How is this different? What needs to change?

How will this programme work with the major gift programme?

Is there a trusts programme?

How will this programme work with the major gift programme?

Programme projects for funding and case for support

Is there an organisational strategic plan that can be shared with donors?

Is there a case for support? How is this agreed internally?

Are there suitable costed projects for major donors to fund?

How are major gifts tracked? Is there certainty the finance is spent where it should be?

Will the finance team offer time and support for the programme? Where are the gaps?

Will there be sufficient programme material, videos and stories to use for touch points with major donors?

Monthly reporting

Is fundraising reported on monthly?

How will the new programme be tracked and reported? How often?

Engagement of senior staff and trustees

Are the chief executive and the leadership willing to commit sufficient time to the programme?

Are leadership willing to be open and accountable to major donors?

Does the programme sit high within the chief executive's list of priorities?

Are leadership committed to restricted giving? Do they realise that most major donors will not want to give to general funds?

Are programme staff willing to assist with donor meetings, write progress reports and share beneficiary stories?

Are trustees aware of the major gift programme? Are they supportive of the programme?

Are trustees willing to meet with major donors?

Do trustees give? Are trustees well connected?

Events
What events do we currently run?
How will this change?

A study such as this builds momentum and 'buy in' within the organisation as staff begin to see how much is involved in its set up, where they fit within the programme, what success might look like and over what time period. It can be an exciting time of planning for all involved and the inclusion of concrete recommendations for the programme as well as the possibility of a decision to not start the programme until the essentials are in place.

The successful executive stakes out the values for the programme

The preparation of a values or philosophy document will underpin your major gift programme. It simply sets out your guidelines for developing relationships with philanthropists. This is particularly needed as the programme touches every department within your organisation – finance, supporter care, communications, programme departments, senior leadership and the trustees.

The purpose of the document is for the organisation to agree shared values of what is important. People often have different ideas about what a 'philanthropy' or major gift programme is, what it entails and how it is run especially when the concept is new. There could be some negative ideas from some members of staff that the programme is 'all about chasing rich people and getting their money'. Nothing could be farther from the truth and therefore the true values of the programme should be written down in the early stages of development.

It is therefore an opportunity for fundraising staff to educate leadership and wider staff and to incite their enthusiasm in this consultative process. It can also appease staff who may have fears that the donor will begin to dictate how the work is carried out. The values document can address how relationships are formed over a long period of time and that donors will only be asked for funding for projects that are already defined, costed and agreed by leadership.

Topics that could be included are:

Why donors give?

What are the key reasons that donors give to your cause? In this section you can include some of the distinctive aspects of your work. It is important to include the point that giving is an opportunity for a donor to express his or her own values. It is not about treating a donor as a cash machine, twisting their arm and persuading them to do something they don't want to do, rather it is about mutual benefit to both parties.

It might include the explanation that a philanthropic donor is given the opportunity to do something significant, and be shown the difference their gift has made. Also the recognition that they give only when asked, when inspired and once they trust the organisation and leadership.

How we work with our donors?

In this section you can include the gift level of entry into the programme. I suggest a minimum of £10,000 per annum per person or couple because of the level of stewardship involved. Other examples are the offering of excellent service, creation of a personal plan for each donor, personal and imaginative thanking, the maintaining of monthly contact, the building of donor memories, keeping of promises and the agreement to maintain contact according to the donor's preference.

The Role of the relationship holder

This will include how the relationship is managed by the major gift executive. For example listening to their interests rather than 'talking at' the donor; answering their questions and objections thoughtfully and showing respect to their views; demonstrating to the donor they matter; sustaining and understanding their motivation; being transparent and honest about shortcomings; applying their gift only to the agreed project; offering specific reports demonstrating the impact their gift has made (some don't like long explanatory documents, others do want the detail!) in a way that is meaningful for the donor.

What donor communication is and what it is not

This section can include key characteristics such as, all communication is 'donor driven' rather than organisation driven; that major donors do not receive direct mail appeals (once qualified into a managed programme) but rather have personalised proposals that match their interest; that respect is shown if a donor does not want to be part of the programme and a donor is allowed to decide their level of involvement without manipulation.

What success looks like and how is it measured

Establishing the criteria for success is important to major gift staff and leadership. Here is an opportunity to declare that success takes time to build and should be measured in years and not just based on finance; it could include the number of meaningful contacts that are made each month steadily moving the programme forward; it could also include something of the responsibility of the executive as 'messenger' and recognition that the gift is entirely at the discretion of each philanthropic donor.

This section could also include more specifics such as, the statement that each donor is asked for a significant gift for a project that matches their interest at least once a year; there is a value of demonstration of courage to approach donors and that the underpinning true core of success is in the authenticity of the relationship that will build year on year; a successful programme will also benefit in ways other than finance as donors may offer advice and skills.

How we use information about our supporters

This will refer to holding information in accordance with regulations. In the UK and EU this needs to comply with the General Data Protection Regulations (GDPR) which is described in more detail in Principle 9. Also bearing in mind that this information can be requested by the donor at any time; that information gleaned from research, meetings and phone calls is recorded accurately and in a timely manner in line with the regulations; that this information will be reviewed before meeting a prospect or major donor and that the information will be selectively used for briefings with internal staff.

An internal processes section may also be added to describe definitions of relationships, for example a process of how the trusts' officer and major gift executive work together; how the major gift executive works with the chief executive to manage relationships; that the executive has the discretion to release major donors back into general support or possibly delete from the database if no interest is shown.

In summary, preparing this philosophy document creates excitement and gives momentum to the programme and brings everyone on board to agree its shared values. It is one of the keys to success.

principle _____ 4

The successful executive sets the minimum gift entry point to the major gift programme at £10,000

The purpose of setting the gift entry point at £10,000 is to set your sights high at the very start of your major gift programme. Research shows that philanthropists want organisations to have vision and, more importantly, to be bold when asking for a gift. The Coutts Million Pound Donor Report demonstrates this:

www.philanthropy.coutts.com

It makes for interesting reading as we see the number of million pound philanthropists growing in the UK. With this increased exposure it is easy to see how this influence can trickle down to wealthy individuals, who give below one million pounds, to feel encouraged to give more.

There is also an increasing trend for wealthy individuals to decide not to support their children with their wealth and instead encourage them to find their own way in life. This in turn means there are more individuals looking for ways to give their money to worthy causes and fulfil their vision of making a difference in the world.

Some fundraisers have suggested the level of gift for entry into a major gift programme should relate to your organisation's level of donations. For some it could be £500 or £1,000, others £5,000 depending on your donors' levels of giving. Others have said 20 times the average gift is the starting point for a major gift programme. However, in all these cases it may be way too low if the donor has a higher £ giving capacity.

If a major gift programme donation entry level is set lower, for example, at £5,000, it can be problematic for a number of reasons. It has been proven many times that if you ask for £5,000, you will receive £5,000 (donors like to please you!). The potential philanthropist may have the £ capacity to give £25,000 if sufficiently motivated, however asking for £5,000 would only achieve £5,000 (again, donors like to please you!). Also bear in mind a major gift executive may only manage to qualify a maximum of 40 ongoing relationships over the first two to three years; if the return was a minimum of £5,000, this equates to a total minimum income of £200,000 and the resultant fundraising return on investment (ROI) is too low to be sustainable.

The £10,000 entry point applies whether you are a small or large organisation. A small organisation can achieve a £10,000 gift from a donor just as easily as a larger organisation. Although, it can be more challenging for a smaller organisation to find a specific £10,000 project for the donor to fund. However, the principles are the same. Therefore why would the level of gift depend on organisation size? Honestly it doesn't. It is much more about finding the right match for the donor's interest.

Setting the minimum at £10,000 raises the bar. It justifies the time required to secure a major gift, both your time and the senior staff time given to meeting with donors. It provides the basis for an improved return on investment (ROI) ratio. It challenges you to think bigger and in turn you will challenge your potential giver to give more and achieve more with their gift, which actually brings more joy and fulfilment.

A philanthropic donor is looking to fund a project that matches his or her own personal values and interests and remarkably, because of your efforts, they have chosen your organisation. Therefore the gift is sizeable and has huge value to your cause. It is a significant and meaningful partnership. They will deeply appreciate your work, will want to get to know you, in many cases will be interested in the detail of why you do what you do and how you do it and, if looked after meticulously by you, will give again and again perhaps for their lifetime. They may in time want to introduce others to your work because of their great experience with you and will perhaps leave a substantial legacy. It is therefore so much more than a simple one-off gift. There is a vast time investment on your part for each significant giver.

For many philanthropic donors it is life changing to see the amazing work their gifts have achieved. Your job is to facilitate this transformational experience for your donor. It doesn't make sense to set your sights on a minimum gift of £5,000.

Picture the Scene.......

Philanthropist Simon: *'Yes I am highly interested in Chile, my work takes me there, and I also used to work there over 20 years ago, I would be delighted to support the development project in Chile.'*

Up until this point the couple had only given gifts of £2,000 and £3,000. The temptation for the executive would be to stretch the gift size to £5,000. Fortunately in this case he challenged the couple to consider way beyond this.

GIVING
Changes Everything

Executive: *'Our cost for this........aspect of the work is £25,000, will you support this?'*

Simon: *'That is a stretch for us, but we'll definitely give it serious thought!'*

The executive took them to visit the work, and of course, they happily donated £25,000. A photo book was made of their visit and presented to them afterwards. This was transformational for the husband in particular. It could have been very different if the challenge, 'the ask', was set at only £5,000.

A gift over £10,000 brings good will to your staff, those you care for, your board who are often astounded by the generosity, your chief executive who will believe in the programme enough to invest more time and money into its success. Most of all, your donor will remember this experience for the rest of his or her life. All round it is a winning programme! Don't ever feel tempted to lower your sights to below £10,000. A new major gift executive may not initially have the confidence to ask for a £10,000+ gift for a number of reasons but it is still more effective to set the standard high and to seek coaching for new inexperienced staff.

Finally, don't feel tempted to gauge gift size on your donor's previous giving. The individual could have given any size gift to your organisation in the past. This could be in the £ thousands or even as low as £20, as on one occasion I remember, had been received from one multi-millionaire. The key point to bear in mind is the individual's potential to give a substantial gift often demonstrated in the research. Do not ever allow yourself to think too small, choosing constantly to challenge yourself to raise your sights. The greater the gift, the greater the joy and excitement it brings to the giver.

Picture the Scene.......

A major gift executive was due to attend an ask meeting with her potential donor who she had known for many months, I asked her:

'How much are you going to ask him to give?'

She answered:
'£5,000, as he gave £4,000 last year'

I challenged her to think about why she was asking for so little as the budget for the project was £30,000 and she knew it was a right match for him.

'Why not ask him to fund the whole project?'

She went with fear and not too little trepidation. Surprise, surprise! He agreed to fund the whole project. It was inefficient to even consider asking for £5,000.

It is possible that a donor may send through an unprompted gift as you are getting to know him or her, for example of £1,000 or £2,000 demonstrating they are enjoying the experience, their relationship with you and catching the vision for your work. This is quite common and a compliment. Don't feel disappointed, immediately thank them very warmly and continue with the relationship. Do not demote them to a mid value programme if they are still showing interest and they have the capacity to give more. You may not yet have found the right project match.

The key issue is that a major gift programme must work financially not only for a good return but also to encourage disbelieving trustees that the programme is worthy of investment, often significant investment. When the 'ask' level is set at a minimum of £10,000 then eventually 40 qualified philanthropic relationships per fundraising executive could achieve over £400,000 per annum. This provides a much more effective return on investment ratio and, of course, is dependent on the ability and training of the executive. The beauty of a major gift programme is the steep fundraising ratio that can be achieved, up to a 1:10 ROI or more as the programme progresses. To achieve this ROI, the aim should always be to raise the bar and set the level high, aiming for a minimum gift size of £10,000.

principle _____5

The successful executive demonstrates the balanced qualities of hunter and nurturer

In this section I wanted to talk about recruitment as well as the qualities required to be a successful major gift executive. Every new programme needs a full-time major gift executive. Please note if you are the recruiter that this is an 'internal title' and not suitable for external use. The role is focused on building long term relationships with the potential major donors on the database. The title for this executive should therefore suggest relationship building rather than include, or even imply, fundraising, gift or donation in the title.

A full-time executive is required to coordinate the major gift work and all approaches to high value donors. It is not advisable to start a programme relying on senior staff to carry out prospecting activities. You need an executive to do this as senior leaders are unlikely to have the time or inclination to assist with donor visits initially except for the very high level ones. Often a senior leader will join the executive on the second meeting after some interest has been established.

If senior leadership team members are not used to participating in major donor work, they will need direction, support and briefing. To try to start a programme without a full-time executive is going to falter from the start. Senior leaders might be excited about their first meeting with a prestigious individual but can lack the time and dedication to nurture and develop the relationship in the weeks and months after the first meeting.

Picture the Scene.......

An organisation was insistent that all relationship building should be done by the senior leaders however they were not organised in their approach to this.

The leaders endured the training reluctantly and did not make time for the work that was involved subsequently. One year later and the programme was no further forward and the financial target had not been met. In fact the senior leaders put pressure on the fundraising staff to bring in the money they had not raised themselves.

Unfortunately there are many organisations employing an executive to undertake random donor and prospect approaches in a purely 'hunting' role. This can appear successful initially, especially if the executive brings in finance, however if the executive leaves there is often no continuity and worse still in some cases they may take the donors with them to their next organisation. Sadly, in this case, when a new member of staff is appointed the programme starts all over again on the same cycle.

What I mean by random approaches is that the donors are not properly researched and ordered according to their likelihood of supporting the cause. The executive randomly approaches, sometimes inappropriate, individuals without continuity frequently asking for a gift too soon, wanting to 'seal the deal' and is often trying new things, approaching those who look the 'wealthiest' even though there is no real connection with the cause.

Picture the Scene.......

An executive was very good at his job. He phoned potential donors, got appointments and brought in finance. However, when I did a review of the programme he was not recording information about his donors, he was shooting from the hip, not introducing the donors to other people within the organisation.

He had no assistant and basically wasn't doing any administration. Rather a loose cannon. He was a nice person, loved travelling round the country seeing donors and on the surface appeared 'successful', however when he left there was not much legacy, we had to start  the programme all over again employing an administrator as well and installing all the processes behind the scenes.

An executive is also needed to oversee setting all the processes in place to ensure the longevity of a major gift programme. However, as a major gift executive, you should be aware there are two essential functions within the role:

1. Securing first meetings with donors on the database, with the aim of qualifying them
2. Managing qualified donors and leading the relationship to a significant 'ask'

These two key functions often create a dilemma for recruiters. The first requires a crisp sales technique with strong persuasion and influencing skills; the second a more nurturing, managing aptitude with careful attention to detail. They are very different qualities.

A salesman will love the hunt and never give up until the donor is courted and brought into the fold. This person will love using the telephone and have belief and high energy for trying to forge new interesting relationships. However, once the donor is qualified and a twelve month plan is in place, the salesman loses interest, becomes bored and instead is ready to chase the next 'difficult to get hold of' donor. If the programme is new, salesmanship qualities are very much needed within a new team for courting philanthropic donors.

By contrast, the nurturers are more cautious by nature and often struggle with phoning strangers. To pick up the phone and contact a business man or woman who is perhaps prickly, time poor and needs persuasion often scares nurturers and they tend to procrastinate this task. This can be evidenced by how few donors have been contacted each month shown by the activity statistics in the monthly report. More about the monthly report is in Principle 36.

However, the nurturer loves to maintain a relationship and will care deeply for the donor and their family and will do everything they can to keep the relationship warm and flowing. A much needed quality for this programme. This characteristic can be evidenced by the number of touch points with 'qualified' donors that have been successfully achieved each month shown on the monthly report statistics.

To be successful you need both. Both are 'people - people'. Both require integrity and determination. However sometimes it can be hard for an executive to balance these two qualities. As an executive, to understand whether your qualities are more appropriate for securing first meetings or perhaps may fit better with managing donors that a more established programme provides, is an important decision to make in order to be successful. It is also important for a recruiter to decide which of these two key qualities is required for the stage at which the programme has arrived. If the new person is taking over a caseload of qualified major donors then a manager, a nurturer of people, is needed.

However, to pioneer a new programme and secure first meetings with donors, salesmanship is needed. As an executive, you need both but the key is where the weighting of your qualities lies. You can develop your skill in the area that you are weakest but to be successful you need to play to your strengths, recognise your key quality and work within that framework.

A radical thought here is the case for recruiting an executive with salesmanship skills to court donors initially and, at a later stage in the programme, recruit a second executive who is responsible for managing the relationships once the donors are qualified. If this process is managed carefully, it is possible for the salesman to handover relationships to an executive with more nurturing qualities. The 'sales' executive may still have some continued contact with the donor occasionally such as when they are invited to visit the office or attend a small lunch. It is not insurmountable to manage this handover and is far more effective than waiting for a nurturer to initiate contact with hard to get hold of donors.

I should add that, as an executive, there are many additional tasks related to these two core functions. These include the ability to:

- Write clearly and succinctly (handwritten notes still have a higher impact over email or typed letters)
- Discern donors' interests and match those interests to a specific project
- Develop and manage those interests
- Prepare budgets and proposals
- Listen carefully and actively
- Present the case in a face to face setting
- Thank creatively
- Demonstrate high emotional intelligence
- Relate well with senior leaders and trustees
- Influence to create a culture of philanthropy within the organisation

Because it can be difficult to locate these skills especially for smaller charities and charities outside London, I like to search for these transferable skills from other roles such as sales and client management. In the recruitment phase using role play, a writing exercise and a one-to-one presentation about a subject the recruit feels passionate about can help track down the required skills. It could be a hobby, family, past time or a charity they support. The questioning in the interview can also help identify these individual qualities.

principle _____ 6

The successful executive always employs a full-time administrator from day one

It is not good stewardship to use your time as a major gift executive to carry out the administration tasks. You need to recruit an administrator at the very beginning of the programme. As the executive you can focus on the 'external' relationship building while the administrator is concentrating on the 'internal' and logistical tasks.

Even a part-time administrator is better than none to assist with all the administrative and 'coordinating' tasks related to:

- List formation
- Ranking donors
- Researching individuals
- Planning
- Compiling a spreadsheet for donor plans
- Writing internal processes
- Refining and cleaning the database
- Interfacing with programme teams to ensure there is a healthy flow of information to pass to donors
- Forming a good case for support
- Preparing the project list
- Keeping the project list up to date
- Costing of programmes for 'asks'
- Preparing first draft proposals for donors and prospects and for 'asks'
- Gathering information for reports and stories to give donors and prospects
- Categorising stories and videos on the shared drive
- Preparing monthly reports for management
- Coordinating the internal liaison
- Arranging meetings, booking travel and accommodation for executives

Of course, as an executive you need to lead on most of these tasks but an administrator can continue the work and see them through under your guidance. There is a big difference between the two roles. You need to be outward facing and the administrator is inward focused. You work closely together. It is poor stewardship to use your time to perform the administrative tasks. In fact the programme will take much longer to establish and is severely hampered by the lack of administrative assistance. You, as the executive, will inevitably become hindered by the internal processes.

Gathering information and costings takes time and if, for example, an information document or proposal takes two days to write, this is very valuable time that you should be using for perhaps meeting with the chief executive to discuss donor plans, telephoning or visiting high level individuals. A skilled administrator can gather the information and compile a first draft for you.

Starting a new programme can sometimes feel like 'wading through treacle' to get things achieved. If you, as the executive are caught up in internal meetings you will not be spending quality time with donors. It also does not play to your skills. If you lead on some of the tasks initially, such as establishing potential projects that donors can fund, your administrator can follow up and hold the detailed process meetings to ensure the end result is achieved to your satisfaction.

In summary, a full time administrator is needed at the beginning of the programme and should be recruited at the same time as the executive if the programme is to have the best chance of success.

The successful executive is realistic about set up costs

Assuming you have been able to lawfully and within data protection regulations (for the UK and EU see Principle 9) identify a sufficient number of multi-millionaires embedded within your database, at least 200 – 400 with a net worth estimated to be over £5 million to £10 million, it is well worth investing in a new major gift programme. The biggest expense for a major gift programme is always staff. In addition to the major gift executive and administrator salaries, a small additional budget is needed. Below is a chart showing a sample budget for an initial programme based on two members of staff, not including salaries:

Item	Budget: dependent on number of wealthy donors and prospects
Travel and subsistence	£5,000 - £8,000
Technical Devices	£3,000
Research	£5,000 - £10,000
Events (very small)	£2,000+
Training	£2,000
Coaching	£5,000 - £8,000
Stationery and printing	£3,000
Total	**£25,000 - £36,000**

Travel and subsistence

The major gift executive will be looking to visit the right donors from the database to qualify on to the programme, therefore a reasonable travel budget is required. For a busy and effective executive you need to allow a minimum of £350 - £500+ each month for travel. Also some allowance for an occasional lunch with prospects or donors and a 'coffee' budget to allow for working in cafes in between meetings with the invaluable wifi access.

Equipment

An executive will need a mobile phone and a laptop. Also a customer relations contact module for the database. These are one-off costs for the first year but allowance should be made in subsequent years for updates and renewals.

Research budget

An initial wealth screening of your database is definitely needed, contracted to an external company (See Principle 9). The screening is free however buying the names that have been identified on your database will require budget. This is a variable amount depending on the size of your database and how many wealthy individuals have been found. Allow £5,000 – £10,000 for this work. It provides the foundation for the programme! An employed prospect researcher is very necessary if there are many wealthy individuals on your database however you can use external companies for some of this research such as Prospecting For Gold. Initially, prospect research can be carried out by your administrator.

Events

Very small lunches can work well to introduce your chief executive or senior leaders to three to four donors at one time, especially if there is common interest. Although, it should be said that very high level individuals need to be met one by one. In fact, you will be fortunate to achieve twenty minutes of their time. Small lunches can be achieved fairly inexpensively especially if hosted in a supporter's board room and with very little executive or administrative time. Allow £2,000 for this first year depending on your plan. It is unlikely you will be in a position to organise much until the latter part of this first year anyway. Just to mention here that larger events are time consuming and not advisable, they in fact divert the major gift staff from their true vocation of building one-to-one relationships.

Training and membership

The executive will need to keep up-to-date and be challenged, so allow £1,000 – £2,000 per annum. Membership of the Institute of Fundraising, if you are in the UK, is important to being able to network and be kept informed. Training courses run throughout the year with the Institute and other bodies such as the Directory of Social Change. Every country will have an institute or similar body that runs local meetings, training courses and conferences.

Coaching

It is really helpful to offer coaching for the executive especially in the first year of the programme. There could be issues of organisational readiness, the case for support not being ready and available, staff not trained, processes not in place to support the programme, long term strategy not available and so on. Allow £5,000 – £10,000 for an external coach. In the end it will save time and money especially if the team is new to major gift fundraising.

Stationery and Printing

This is a minimal cost initially. Glossy brochures are not required to start a programme but small amounts are needed for stamps for handwritten envelopes, quality stationery, presentable crockery for donor visits to the office, simple invitations for small events and thank you cards to donors.

Your initial investment is therefore approximately £100,000 for the first year. The total is the costs outlined above plus a full-time executive and full-time administrator/prospect researcher.

By investing sufficiently at the beginning of the programme, it can grow quickly and will give confidence to senior leadership and the trustees. You are more likely to succeed if you invest substantially upfront rather than 'behind the curve'. Setting up the programme is hard work but will be worthwhile and will pay dividends over time.

principle   8

The successful executive starts a processes file from day one

A processes file is simply a place where you write down everything you do within the programme and the method. This can be simple bullet points to describe each task. As you start a new programme you are constantly developing new tasks and ways of doing them and these need to be diligently recorded in an easy to read format. Each task has its own simple description of the process. The file is usually overseen and managed by the administrator.

Over time the file will grow in size. Most people keep this file electronically on the shared drive however there is great merit in also keeping a hard copy in your team's office space. Every new process can be segmented by subject and have a separate page for easy reference. It makes for quite a bulky, hard copy file and not every team wants to do this but it is freely available for reference and it does raise its importance and visibility.

The processes file is building longevity into the programme. It is the difference between a random programme and a long term sustainable programme that grows year on year. You are building for the future. If a member of staff leaves, their tasks are already written up as processes within the file. It is also very helpful as a reference library for a new member of staff. Not exactly bedtime reading but readily accessible as needed. A task's process can be looked up at any time.

The processes should cover everything such as how donors are thanked at each gift level, within what time frame and who is responsible. The tasks can vary from 'how you thank a donor who has given a gift over £25,000', which is likely to involve the chief executive in the thanking process, to how to research and decide whether a donor is suitable for the major gift programme. It will also include the style guide for writing to major donors, for example the inclusion of the use of live stamps and quality envelopes.

Here is an example of the contents of one team's processes file that is still in the development stage:

- How to search for new wealthy donors
- How donors are profiled
- How to request research on a donor (major gift executive to prospect researcher)
- Performing due diligence
- What is a qualified donor?
- How to qualify a donor
- How to unqualify a donor
- Definition of an 'active' donor
- Definition of the RAG (red amber green) status for donors
- Definition of the RAG (red amber green) status for qualified caseload donors
- What to do when a cheque is received
- How a donor sends funds by bank transfer
- Process for web donations
- How to allocate income on the database
- How to claim gift aid from a donor
- Style guide for thanking donors
- Style guide for writing to donors
- Process for thanking
- Process for chief executive to thank
- The project list
- Project proposals
- Project reports - what to expect and when
- How to request additional project information
- How to find and use branding
- Use of the quarterly magazine
- Christmas cards
- How to upload a video on to YouTube
- IT troubleshooting
- Collating donor names for the annual report

- How to record data
- Process for an office visit (Red Carpet Day which is described in more detail in Book Two)

In summary it is the written detail of every task in the programme. It is best written in simple, plain English in a bullet point format that is easy to read. It is not a time consuming, major task that the administrator has to undertake but rather a slow build of notating 'what we do' and 'how we do it' so that everyone is clear and working on the same agreed principles. 'Additions to the processes file this month' could be added to the agenda at every monthly team meeting. The administrator can be noting what to add to the processes file during the meeting as new decisions are made.

This is a continual piece of work for the administrator to constantly update. It is reassuring for the team and builds a successful programme that will continue to grow from strength to strength.

The successful executive seeks out the multi-millionaires on the database

Finding the multi-millionaires embedded within your data is an exciting first step and often leadership and trustees are amazed at the results. It is quite common for leadership to assume there are no wealthy individuals on their database because no large gifts have been received by the organisation.

Picture the Scene.......

I can recall many conversations that have taken place where senior leadership are deeply surprised at how many multi-millionaires are embedded within their database. Usually the conversation plays out something like this:

Director: *'No, I am convinced that there are no wealthy supporters on our system, our supporters are mostly those who give smaller donations in response to our newsletters and appeals.'*

Later, after receipt of the wealth screening results from an external source:

Consultant: *'The results show that you have 432 millionaires and multi-millionaires in your listing'*

Director: *'What?? We need to rethink this'*

A donor is very unlikely to give a large gift unless the proposal offered fits within their own personal goals and interests. If there has not been a major gift programme in the past then it is unlikely the donor has been offered an appropriate proposal that matches their interest. It is more likely they may have only given a small gift in response to a direct mail piece which suggests interest but nothing to really excite them. This is the reason why a philanthropic major donor could be on your database but has not chosen to give a sizeable gift. This is quite common.

The ability to wealth screen has come into the spotlight in the UK by the Information Commissioner's Office (ICO) who is enforcing the General Data Protection Regulations (GDPR). If you are based in the UK or the EU, your wealth screening needs to be compliant with the General Data Protection Regulations (May 2018). You can refer to the Information Commissioner's Office (ICO) website for the most recent codes of practice on data protection to ensure that your wealth screening is carried out lawfully. Other countries are likely to have similar codes. To help you to understand and apply this, I have added a section at the end of this Principle written by Andrew Barton, Independent Consultant and former Fundraising Director at Oxfam, Great Britain, together with some useful reading.

It is advisable to ask an outside specialist company to screen your database for wealthy individuals such as Prospecting For Gold Limited in the UK. The results give confidence for the leadership and trustees to have the determination to set up a new programme. A wealth screening will identify how many millionaires and multi-millionaires are within your database.

There is usually no charge to have the first screening undertaken. You will receive a summary of the number of millionaires, although not their names, embedded within your database. A typical result is between 1% and 3% of the data submitted. For example, if you submit data consisting of 20,000 names to a prospect research company, they are highly likely to find between 200 and 600 millionaires and multi-millionaires within your database. Or if your database of supporters is 2,000, you might expect to find 20 – 60 millionaires and multi-millionaires.

Ideally to get the best result, give the entire database to the company including non givers, volunteers, council of reference, trustees and names within all groups associated with your organisation, particularly those who have been active within the past five years. This will give you the widest potential list and the most comprehensive start to knowing how many wealthy individuals are already connected to your cause.

Commissioning a wealth screening is really worth the investment as it forms the basis for your programme, the foundation for everything you do. It will be very difficult to start a major gift programme without it. It could cost anything from £3,000 - £10,000 to purchase the names identified from the wealth screening depending on how many names are found. There is no short cut to this and it is worth every £ investment at this early stage.

There are five major categories of wealth usually used by researchers. The wealth screening will give you the numbers of individuals within these wealth categories:

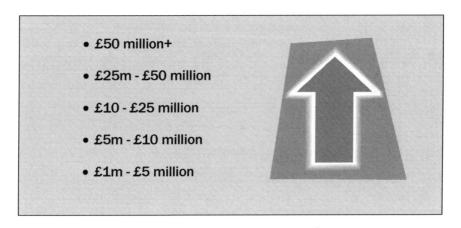

- £50 million+
- £25m - £50 million
- £10 - £25 million
- £5m - £10 million
- £1m - £5 million

These figures refer to an individual's personal wealth not including their main place of residence. As wealthy individuals often have multiple residences, this rarely can be an exact science. However a specialist research company collect data on wealthy individuals and will match your data with their data and will give you an indication into which category each donor or prospect falls. They will also include age bands, and whether the wealthy individual in the household is the one on your database. Depending on how much you are willing to pay for each name, you can also find out more detail, for example, whether they have a £1million+

property or are:

- Charity Trustee
- Donor
- Company Director
- PLC Director
- FTSE 350 Director
- Grant Making Trustee
- Influential
- Established Money
- Livery Company
- Member National Gardens Scheme
- VCT Investor (high risk venture capitalist)

Your best donors and prospects for a major gift programme will generally fall between the £5 million to £50+ million categories although sometimes there are generous individuals found within the £1million to £5million category. Your wealth screening will indicate how many individuals you have within each of these categories. These names should then be ranked as described in Principle 10 and form the basis for your major gift programme.

Wealth screening and profiling lawfully

Although the following advice applies to the UK and EU, other countries may have similar regulations. Please note that it also applies if your organisation is looking to approach a philanthropic major donor residing in the UK or EU.

There needs to be a valid legal basis for each purpose for processing your data.

There are 6 legal bases under the GDPR, however in fundraising there are really only 2 out of the 6 practical alternatives: Consent and Legitimate Interest.

If you wish to conduct wealth screening and prospect research profiling there needs to be a legal basis for these specific purposes of processing.

You don't need to have the same legal basis for all purposes for your data processing. Even if you have decided to go down a Consent approach for direct marketing with existing supporters such as Cancer Research UK and the Royal National Lifeboat Institute have done, you may decide to use Legitimate Interest as your basis for wealth screening and profiling.

There are some pre-requisites for Legitimate Interest to be an acceptable basis for wealth screening and profiling. You need to:

- Offer donors the chance to opt-out of direct marketing.
- Offer a clear statement of how to opt-out of wealth screening and profiling in the privacy statement.
- Update your privacy policy that explains your different legal bases for processing. As an example some universities in the UK have covered wealth screening and profiling particularly well on their websites.
- Clearly communicate in your supporter communications that there is a new privacy policy in place and highlight wealth screening and profiling.
- Write a 'balancing assessment' for wealth screening and profiling preferably signed off by someone who does not have direct line accountability for fundraising.

Overall, you need to keep up-to-date with advice and guidance from both the Fundraising Regulator (FR) and the ICO in the UK and EU remembering that the FR can decide to have a higher standard than the legal requirement in its Code of Fundraising Practice.

Further useful reading to ensure you are compliant if you are based in the UK and EU can be found in the following documents:

Institute of Fundraising:
"GDPR: The Essentials for Fundraising Organisations"
 - in partnership with Bircham Dyson Bell
"11 steps to your consent and permissions" - A fast.MAP guide
Bird & Bird:
"Guide to the GDPR"

Data Protection Network:
"Guidance on the use of Legitimate Interests under the EU GDPR"
Fundraising Regulator:
"Personal Information and Fundraising: Consent, Purpose and
 Transparency" - in partnership with Protecture
ICO:
"Preparing for the GDPR - 12 steps to take now"
"Consultation: GDPR consent guidance"
"Privacy Notices, Transparency and Control"

principle_____10

The successful executive ranks their donors and prospects

Your first task after the wealth screening is completed is to place all wealthy donors and prospects into a logical order. The most effective way of deciding who to approach first is to rank them. This gives structure to your programme. This is often referred to as a 'ranking list'. It is important that every name from the wealth screening result as well as all other philanthropic major donors and prospects are included. If there is one central list it avoids the confusion of having lots of different lists, worse still, you might leave someone out. I have known organisations that have different lists for different purposes but it often leads to confusion. Ideally, there should be one centralised, 'master' list.

This should be automated by a report from the data on your database into a spread sheet. If the expertise is not available in house, then use an outside resource to help you achieve this. An example is Gareth Williams at UK Prospect Research Ltd, who is excellent and will help you establish the reports you need. The report needs to be run regularly and constantly refined as new donors and prospects are added. Some organisations run this report every few days as the numbered ranking order changes every time a new name is added. Others run the report once a month, really it's up to you to decide how frequently.

The reason for the ranking list is that it is important to recognise engagement with your organisation as well as wealth. For example an individual with a personal wealth of £50 million who has very little linkage to your organisation may not be the first person to approach. In fact, it may be that they appear much lower down on the ranking list. You may be able to build a more successful relationship with a couple with a £5m to £10m wealth band who have given small gifts over recent years. In summary, you need to look for the wealthiest and the most engaged. Those who have both these characteristics will score more highly.

It is best practice to keep your first ranking list simple and very easy to keep up-to-date. More detailed desk research as to a donor's ability to make a high level gift can be found at the next stage once they have been qualified. Initially you are looking for the likely probability that a donor can potentially give a £10,000+ gift to your organisation and has demonstrated an interest in your work.

The role of the ranking list is therefore to order your work and to take account of those who are the:

- Wealthiest
- Most engaged with your organisation
- Most supportive over the longest time period
- Most generous (use of a **recency** – when did they last give, **frequency** – how often have they given and **value** – what size £ gifts have they given, calculation)
- Most connected with your staff

Those who are not as warm to your cause will take much longer to build a relationship with and some may never prove to be significant donors. It is a waste of your time and the donor's time to spend valuable man hours cultivating those who are quite distant to your cause.

Picture the Scene.......

Here is a real example of how valuable prospecting time was lost.

...and the Oscars go to...

Head of Fundraising: *'I see you have logged a lot of time against our prospect, the actor, Jeremy Billions'*

Executive: *'Yes, our research found him to have a personal wealth of £750 million! I have spent a lot of time attending his events, speaking with his PA, and trying to get closer and closer'.*

...... Continued over

> **Head of Fundraising: Have you been able to discuss our charity's work with him?**
>
> **Executive: Well last time I was actually able to get through, he told me he wasn't really interested in what we do but I am sure he will come round.**
>
> **Head of Fundraising: 'Hmmm. Is that the best use of your prospecting time?'**

Sometimes it is easy to be over optimistic as to who will respond and spend too much time chasing a dream that won't come true. That is why a ranking list of donors and prospects will really help to prioritise.

In its simplest scoring form you can award 5 points to each of the categories making a total score of 25: The wealthiest, longevity of support, most generous, most engaged and most connected with staff.

Wealthiest

For example the wealth can be ranked as follows:

Wealth Band	Score
£50 million +	5
£25 - £50 million	4
£10 - £25 million	3
£5 - £10 million	2
£1 - £5 million	1

I prefer to give the higher ranks to those most likely to be a philanthropic major donor. It seems rather 'upside down' to give the lowest scores to the wealthiest donors.

Longevity of support

Similarly you can score in a similar way for the longest time period supporting your cause.

Time supporting	Score
15 – 20 years	5
10 – 14 years	4
6 – 9 years	3
3 – 5 years	2
0 – 2 years	1

However this category is only relevant to use if you have records on your database going back for 10 - 15+ years. You need to adjust the scoring and years according to your data. If your database is fairly new then this category may not be as useful. Already with these two characteristics, you have a score out of 10 for each donor or prospect.

Most generous

Next you can score donation history which demonstrates those who have been most generous. It is likely the gifts will be lower as most major donors will not yet have given a major gift, however it can still demonstrate those who have shown interest enough to have given gifts over many years. The scoring is often linked to lifetime value of giving.

Most engaged with your organisation

The score for warmth is individual to your organisation. It is determined by what information is retained on your database. Examples might be: has a monthly/regular direct debit or standing order, receives an 'opt-in' newsletter, has attended an event, is known by a member of staff, the list is endless. These tend to be actions that a supporter has in some way taken with your organisation and, most importantly, the information is held on the database. You can award a point for each attribute.

Most connected with your staff

Connections to your staff and trustees can also be ranked although in my experience it is quite rare for staff or trustees to know many of the prospective major donors on the database. Although for some more regional organisations, leadership and staff often have greater connection with donors. Occasionally there is a surprise, therefore it is definitely worth asking who knows who.

Picture the Scene.......

I remember once talking to a junior member of staff in the kitchen while we were getting coffee. As we were talking, she casually mentioned that her sister went to school with the daughter of a well known multi-millionaire philanthropist who had a significant charitable trust.

Exclamations of '*What!!!!*' and spilling of coffee followed.

'*You haven't told me this before*'.

It resulted in a £20,000 first gift from the philanthropist's trust.

Major gift teams approach ranking their donors and prospects in slightly different ways. The result you want to avoid on your ranking list is having too many individuals scoring at the same level so you may need to add in more criteria to order your list one by one rather than having, for example, 50 with the same score. To achieve this you can begin to unpack the data more. One organisation weighted the scoring system, rather than just giving each criteria one point. For example, if the donor had a direct debit with the organisation, they awarded five points. Another organisation had 10 actions in the most engaged category. It was therefore possible for an individual to score a maximum of 10 in that one category.

However you need to be careful that the wealthiest don't end up ranked at the bottom of the list. If you rank the most generous category too heavily you will be excluding some of the wealthiest. A balance between most engaged and wealth is what you are aiming for. In major gift work the most engaged factor is often called the 'propensity' to give, that is the likelihood of the donor to give to your organisation.

Another charity looked at liquid wealth and investments and scored this additionally. Others have included how many children and whether they have left home to indicate more liquid wealth. You need to find what works best for you and most importantly use the profile that is **held on your database** and come up with your own efficient ranking system. The report has to be generated automatically and therefore the criteria used for the exercise has to be held on your database against each donor or prospect.

The aim is to put all your wealthy donors and prospects into one central ranking list. This provides some strategy as to who you should approach first, who next and so on. The key part is to start contacting donors in a logical order and not spend too many hours setting up and maintaining the ranking list!

Examples of Ranking Lists

An example of a ranking list can be downloaded in colour from my website at the following address:

www.ascentphilanthropy.co.uk under 'Resources'

Notice in Ranking List One that those at the top have scored highly in £ capacity, donations and history. The wealth bandings can also be colour coded so you can see at a glance which contact has the greatest wealth capacity. For example, £50 million+ individuals could be red, £25 to £50 million orange and £5 to £10 million yellow.

Colours in the final column can be used to show who is managing the relationship. The H/I column refers to whether the wealthy individual is living in the household (H) with the wealthy individual, for example a wife or husband, or whether the name on your database is the wealthy individual. For example it is quite common to have the wife's name on your charity's database but the wealth band refers to the husband and his earnings. Or the other way round.

The source column refers to how the name was recognised as a major donor. Initials can be added that are relevant for your organisation. It refers to the source from where you first heard the donor was wealthy. For example, it could be the prospect research company, your own research work internally or recommendations from trustees.

Another ranking list example is also at the following address:

www.ascentphilanthropy.co.uk under 'Resources'

Notice that in Ranking List Two the ranking score for the highest prospect is 97. The lowest score shown at row 22 on the ranking list has a score of 72. These are much higher scores than the previous example. This example also includes highest gift and most recent gift. This is a national charity with a database of hundreds of thousands and therefore does warrant a more sophisticated ranking system. In summary, donors, qualified donors and prospects should appear on the ranking list. There is no need to keep them on separate lists. It is much simpler and easier to maintain only one master ranking list.

principle_____11

The successful executive distinguishes clearly between prospective major donors and their qualified caseload donors

When you first begin a major gift programme it is likely that most of the prospective major donors identified in the wealth screening from your database are individuals who have shown some interest in the past but have not yet given a significant gift. Some have given smaller gifts but not all. They are still prospects for major gifts, albeit they may have given a token gift in the past, and therefore you don't yet know which of them will be engaged enough to your organisation to decide they would like to become further involved and eventually develop into a significant giver.

There is a world of difference between how you engage with a philanthropist who you 'hope' will be interested in your cause but hasn't shown much interest thus far, and a how you manage a committed philanthropist who, through your conversation, has demonstrated to you an interest in your work and has a desire to find out more. The latter is almost ready to be qualified.

Over the years I have observed this as one of the most notable areas of confusion. It is important to have a clear distinction between potential major donors (many are current smaller givers) and your qualified caseload donors. In almost every case when I first begin training a major gift executive, they will have the two mixed together within the same list. It sounds simple but it can be difficult to clearly differentiate between prospective major donors and qualified caseload donors. Once you can clearly distinguish between the two you will begin to make significant progress.

Let's look at the difference. When you first approach a potential major donor from your database, identified in the wealth screening, there are only three possible outcomes:

1. You have spoken to them, they are interested and willing to find out more – this person can be considered for your qualified caseload
2. You have spoken to them, they show no interest, therefore you do not pursue them
3. You tried hard but can't make contact

Let's talk more about outcome 3 as many individuals on your database fall into this category. You have tried to contact them but the telephone number is ex-directory. You have emailed or sent a personal, hand written letter and they haven't responded. You have looked for a connection with another donor, a trustee or a staff member and there is no obvious link. You may ask yourself, what can I do at this point to make contact with this 'hard to get hold of' person? Are they interested in our cause?

One possibility is to dig into your desk research and try to locate on which committees they serve. If you research their name and their village or town, you may find some possibilities and you may discover a link with another donor, trustee or member of staff.

It is possible the only viable telephone number you may have is their work number if you have discovered their place of employment. Your role as a major gift executive is to make contact and thank them if they have given before, tell them something about the exciting work you are doing and see if there is a match of interest. Remember that this programme is based on donor choice and each person has the choice as to whether they would like the relationship to continue or not. Always bear in mind that you are just the messenger. You are not responsible for the outcome.

I have also found that their email address may be located on their company's website and this again is an excellent method of contact. LinkedIn is also an optional way to make contact with an individual.

Picture the Scene.......

When I was trying to make contact with a senior level individual in the City, I found a write up about him and his email address on his company's website, it took all of two minutes!! I tried emailing him. Amazingly, he responded within twenty minutes. Although he was on the database, he was keen and interested to know why our organisation was contacting him. This lead on to a first meeting. When we met he kept asking *'How did you get my email address?'* He clearly didn't know it was on his bank's website, which is quite amusing really. He was very keen to get to know us better.

Unfortunately, it doesn't always go so well. I remember phoning one individual at work and thanking him for his

interest. He was obviously having a bad day and said *'I am not interested, in fact I haven't even heard of you, why are you calling me?'* At some point in the past he must have had contact with our organisation to be on the database but clearly couldn't remember anything about

this. As you can imagine I didn't get very far and removed him from our list.

It is important to keep prospective major donors and qualified caseload donors on separate pages on the relationship chart and not mix them together. Qualified caseload donors require far more time and commitment. Detail on the criteria for qualification is in Principle 15. Further information on the use of a relationship chart spreadsheet for the twelve month plan is described in more detail in Principle 30.

principle _____ 12

The successful executive focuses on a limited number of prospective major donors

At the beginning of the prospecting phase an executive needs a minimum of 30 'active' prospective major donors selected from the top section of the ranking list together with the research on each person. These are donors who you are beginning to actively approach, hence the word 'active'. Every donor needs to be qualified even if they have given before. It is better to have a smaller number, ideally 30 to 40, and focus on trying to get through to them before expanding this 'active' list. As you make contact and either qualify or unqualify some you can keep adding more but keep the total list to around 30 or so. If you have too many, it is easy for you to spread yourself too thin and not achieve even one qualification.

It is helpful to define 'active' to help clarify your task. Otherwise it can seem quite random and out of control. Here is an example of one team's definition for 'active' prospective major donors that could be added to your processes file as described in Principle 8.

'ACTIVE' PROSPECTIVE MAJOR DONOR DEFINITION

These are pre-qualification donors and prospects who have the ability to give £10,000+ in one gift with whom the major gift executive is actively working to qualify:

- They could be a previous donor or a non-donor prospect
- They have been referred by the prospect researcher from the ranking list or from a research company with an accompanying profile

- They are recorded on the 'prospective major donor' page of the relationship chart spreadsheet, see Principle 30
- A two to three month plan is in place on the spreadsheet
- Monthly touch points are executed **every** month for **every** 'active' prospective major donor
- There is a minimum time of three months and maximum time of six months to qualify
- All contact activity and notes are recorded on the database
- Ideal number is approximately 30 to 40 which represents engaging with 30 to 40 prospective major donors monthly

It is so important that you attempt to contact every person every month if they are on your 'active' list. The worst scenario is to try contacting an individual, not get through, and then just leave it for two to three or more months.   Worse still if you have sent a letter saying you would be in contact and then not following up on this. I have found this happens so often. Either the executive gets bored with making calls and becomes disheartened or becomes distracted with other donors.

If a prospective major donor is on your 'active' list, you need to stay active with them. If, after six months, you still haven't been able to make meaningful contact, even though you have consistently tried, then take them off your 'active' list. At least until you have just cause to add them back into your 'active' list, perhaps because they give a donation. I would not advise you to hold on to an 'active' list that is getting longer, definitely not over 40.   It is depressing for you and it will definitely feel out of control.

Very occasionally there will be exceptions. For example, the donor lives abroad, has a high £ capacity and the plan indicates waiting for the right connection which will take longer than six months. Another example might be that you do have a connection and you are waiting for a specific action between your connection (could be, for example, a trustee or another committed donor) and the donor. Even in this latter case though, I would be gently urging your connection to act.

Prospecting should be a continuous rolling programme that requires keen executive discernment as to the best use of time, with donors being moved off the 'active' page by the executive within the six month period because they are:

- Qualified by the executive and added to their caseload
- Returned to prospect researcher (with reason given) in order to:
    o Return to potential major donor pool
    o Return to general direct marketing pool
- Replaced with higher ranking prospective major donors received from the prospect researcher from the ranking list

The key message is don't hold on to prospective major donors for too long. Six months is a good guideline. By that time, if you have had regular contact, you should have a good idea whether they are likely to continue the relationship with you or not. If not get the donor put back into other programmes where they will be better served and your time isn't wasted. However interesting a wealthy donor or prospect might be, if they are not interested in your cause, it is not worth your time pursuing them.

The 'active' prospective major donor page on the relationship chart should be live and rolling. As donors are rolled off, they are replaced with new names advised from the prospect researcher.

principle _____ 13

The successful executive researches every prospective major donor on their 'active' list

After an 'active' list has been chosen from the donors and prospects near to the top of the ranking list who have scored highly in the ranking criteria, the first task is for the prospect researcher to produce a profile on each person required for addition to the executive's 'active' list.

It is important to note here that prospect research is not and never has been illegal. The key to remember is that you must meet the requirements of the General Data Protection Regulations (May 2018) in the EU and UK or the data protection regulations for your country, to enable you to lawfully undertake these activities. For further details refer to Principle 9.

Your privacy notice should make it clear that you may engage in prospect research in order to better understand your donors and that you have a legitimate interest to do so to support your fundraising programme. If you have any doubt as to how to write this notice, refer to the excellent information provided by the Institute of Fundraising and other bodies as listed in Principle 9.

Here is an example of a basic profile. A photo can sometimes be found from the place of work website. This consists of basic information that can be found through publicly available information from the internet:

Donor Profile example

Full name /names	George John Brown (1394061) & Harriett Brown
Address	Sycamore House, Long Brickhill, Buckinghamshire MK82 6AQ, United Kingdom
Phone/Email/Mob	01425 9460 8011 **george.brown@brown-telecom.co.uk** 03832 6744982
Date of Birth	20/9/62
Ranking List	Ranking = 59 Score = 18

Giving	
Largest gift	£1000 04/11/15
Lifetime giving	£10,110.27
Last gift	£600 03/10/17
Regular Gift:	No
Mailings: All Mail	
Giving method: Cheque / CAF	
Family: Twins – Emily and Harold	
Education: Harrow	
Other Charity interests: Shaftsbury, Save the Children	

Directorships	
Birchester Greenhouses Selling beautiful greenhouses	
Perfect Trading Ltd Sale of internet 'perfect presents'	
G J Brown & Associates Ltd Telecom equipment and systems	
T E Holdings	

Wealth £5m - £10m
Motivations and interests: Campaigning, local church, cycling
Organisation Interests:
Trustee of:
Property in Buckinghamshire –   **House value (est) £1.25 million**

The initial prospect research helps the executive get started by providing basic information for the initial 30 to 40 'active' prospective major donors. This information can be found by using many different tools on the web to locate house price, where the person works, if they have a role in the local community, their directorships and charitable activity. Beginning the research with their name and postcode will often start the research process. There are many internet tools that can be used such as Mouse Price, Bing and Dogpile in the United Kingdom. These are constantly being updated.

It is also possible to subscribe to a research company for a quicker download of this information. Research is a time consuming task and a prospect researcher needs to support the major gift executive from the beginning as the programme is being established.

Who to qualify into your major gift programme is a big decision. It is really is important to use research to justify that an individual has the capability, or at least the potential, to give a gift over £10,000. This is not an exact science and you or your prospect researcher will need to dig through the research to make a best guess.

principle_____14

The successful executive doesn't prejudge a donor

One of the lessons I learned early on in my career was not to prejudge a donor. Honestly, it really is true that the individuals you think can't possibly be interested in your organisation often **are** and others who appear as a 'natural match' to your organisation may have **no interest** at all.

Your time is your most precious commodity and you cannot pursue hundreds of prospective major donors. At some stage, some of your donors will become your most generous philanthropists. Do not prejudge who that will be. You truly don't know until you begin approaching them one by one.

Picture the Scene.......

I remember a lady who appeared on the 'active' prospect list, who lived quite simply with no obvious sign of wealth. She was particularly interested in one specific country in South America. However she was a stickler for detail. She wanted every question answered, literally every 'I' dotted and 'T' crossed before giving. Although this was rather arduous in terms of getting all her questions answered, she was fabulously generous and gave £100,000 to the project!! This is a perfect example of not pre-judging which of your donors will give generously.

I caN BEE GENEROUS by sharing freely.

Sometimes you may hesitate to telephone a donor because you have prejudged why they won't be interested. Be disciplined and train yourself not to do this. Attack each one of your donors with equal vigour and enthusiasm.

Picture the Scene.......

Another example is a couple who had a particular interest in a project that was related to marriage work. They also didn't have the obvious trappings of wealth. After building the relationship, I went to talk with them about funding a new marriage project for £24,000, thinking they would contribute a gift towards this. I asked them to fund the whole project – nothing ventured, nothing gained................. they said 'yes' straightaway. I was quite shocked. I shouldn't have prejudged that they weren't capable of or interested enough to do this.

Work hard at not waiting too long to call a donor with excuses such as, 'they could be at lunch; they could be in a meeting; it's too early; it's too late; I'll wait until they have received the newsletter'. There are endless reasons to procrastinate. The truth is there is never a 'best time to call' because what works for one person probably won't work for the next. We waste too much time prejudging and doubting ourselves and our ability to engage donors. My best advice is do not think too much, as all that 'prejudging time' could be spent having great conversations with donors.

Of course every donor needs a prepared script to give you fluency. Have in front of you brief notes on your opening statements usually couched in thanks for their past or many gifts, a brief history of their relationship with your charity and a reason for calling but have these easily available and keep trying people at different times of day. Find a way to keep these notes close to you all the time as, if on that rare occasion a donor calls you back, you don't want to be caught off guard. As described in Principle 12, you are likely to have an ongoing list of 30 to 40 people you are trying to get through to. Do not prejudge and choose who to contact first, just keep trying them all in equal measure.

Often the most difficult part of a major gift executive's job is trying to qualify donors. I would suggest that you try and make light of it, enjoy it, don't prejudge and allow yourself to be surprised! Do your homework and don't specify times when you take a deep breath and 'will now phone all your key donors and prospects'. Have your telephone lists with you wherever you are. Keep trying them when you are travelling, if reception allows, before or after a meeting, first thing in the morning, just before you go home, in the evening, any time you have a gap.

Don't over think it. Definitely don't waste time prejudging and, as a final point, always have the next touch point secured before you finish the phone call. Just keep going, keep enthusiastic and you will succeed!

principle_____15

The successful executive decides the criteria for qualifying a donor

It is a big decision for the major gift executive to decide who to qualify and at what point in the relationship to qualify them. As you approach your donors and get closer to them you begin to understand their interests and motivations and you are looking for those who are showing an interest in you, your organisation and are willing to journey with you and find out more. These are the ones who are ready to be qualified.

It is helpful to look for signs of engagement. A qualified donor will have:

- Had a face to face meeting with the major gift executive at least once
- Shown interest and asked questions; they are alert, engaged and responding warmly
- Shown interest in at least one particular aspect of your organisation's work
- Have demonstrated an interest in similar charities (you have asked what other charitable interests they have)
- Shown willingness to engage further, agreed the next action
- Shown the capability to give over £10,000 in one gift, that is, they appear to have the resources to give

It is not easy to ascertain whether an individual or couple have the ability to give your organisation a significant gift. However a decision has to be made as to whether to invest significant time in developing the relationship. If you have studied the research on their background and current job and can make an assessment of their potential liquidity when you visit them, it will help you form a decision. It is not an exact science. I have been surprised many times over the years. If they have signs of wealth and are enthusiastic about your work, you can only move forward in faith that they will choose to give significantly in the future.

Once you have qualified a person you are committed to building a life time relationship with that person and your organisation. It's a big step. Think of your qualified caseload donors as royalty, those who will have your undivided attention. Prospective major donors are 'in waiting' but haven't made it yet.

Your qualified caseload is prestigious because your aim is to make it meaningful, if not transformational, for the potential giver. Remember that a significant giver is a satisfied, joyful giver. They will be delighted if they can give to something specific and see lives changed as a result.

Once they are qualified the commitment to stewarding this potential investor in your cause includes:

- Monthly communication sometimes more
- Memorising previous conversations before a meeting
- Listening to every word spoken so you truly know them
- Listening to them, understanding their values and trying to match their values with your organisation's mission
- Meeting their need to offer something valuable to the world
- Answering their questions and objections
- Communicating with them in their preferred way
- Remembering every detail about their family
- Engaging with their family, pet, hobby
- Regular travel time to their home and office
- Organising a visit to your office ('Red Carpet Day'- see Book Two)
- Introducing them to your chief executive and programme directors who will answer their detailed questions and speak about the vision
- Facilitating the building of a relationship with your directors
- Enlightening their interest with personally written information and pictures

- Choosing and showing video pieces that fit their interest
- Allowing them to journey with you at their pace
- Preparing a twelve month plan of touch points including the 'ask'
- Forecasting how much they might give and which month
- Entering this into your team's £ forecast for the year
- Making the 'ask' (preferably a 3 – 5 year commitment) when you have demonstrated the need and believe the potential philanthropist is ready and wanting to give
- Preparing a personal project proposal that fits their interest and passion and at the right price
- Stewarding the donor, showing the difference they have made through regular thanking and feedback
- Continuing monthly contact after the gift has been made and building a further twelve month plan towards their second gift
- Taking them to visit the project they are supporting, or might consider supporting

This is a huge commitment on your part and therefore I would think very hard before qualifying a person in to this illustrious group. One of the key success factors for major gift executives is knowing where to focus your time and energy. It's important that you don't give your best time to people who aren't going to ultimately engage with you in the way that you want them to. Obviously there is some element of risk in this decision but do all you can to ensure it's a calculated risk by only qualifying those who are responding and demonstrating signs of engagement.

Prospecting requires patience and determination. It is a 'hunting' role. It may take two to three months just to get an appointment which may be for only twenty minutes. However this can often be enough time to begin a long term mutually beneficial relationship with your organisation.

principle_____16

The successful executive keeps their qualified caseload of donors small and manageable

It is likely that only one out of three donors from your 'active' list, described in Principle 12, will go forward to be qualified. Donors have choice and your organisation may not be the one they choose to become further involved with or want to give a major gift to, even though they may have given a gift in the past.

This in turn means that two out of three prospective major donors you speak to will most likely not want to pursue the relationship. This is normal. That is fine. If they are not interested let them go. It can be painful sometimes if they are wealthy and philanthropic but do not waste your time trying to persuade a disinterested person. The exciting part is that one in three does want to find out more!

A great deal of time is spent developing each relationship as described in Principle 15. You therefore need to steward your time working towards qualifying a caseload of 30, and at the very outside no more than 40, who are giving an annual gift in excess of £10,000. Most executives I work with reach their full working capacity with a qualified caseload of approximately 30 individuals. The only exception might be if your average major gift is exceptionally high, for example over £50,000, in which case it is likely an executive can only manage 20 qualified donors on their caseload.

It might take two to three years to eventually qualify a caseload of around 30 but it is so important to keep focused and not fill your qualified caseload with people who take a lot of your time but don't give at the right level and aren't sufficiently interested to warrant your time.

If you qualify more than 30 donors (maximum 40) and thereby end up spending less quality time with each person or couple, inevitably the experience will be less rewarding for the donor and the gift will be lower.

Some organisations find that a qualified caseload may only need 30 individuals for a high return. If each of those individuals is highly involved with you and giving at significant levels over £10,000, then a caseload of approximately 30 will be the right number to manage. One organisation I worked with had an average gift of £43,000 (many giving at the £10,000 level and others more) from their significant givers and the major gift executive managed a caseload of only 32 individuals.

Just to say again, it is absolutely fine if you know that an individual has the £ capacity and is therefore capable of giving a significant gift but only gives £5,000 as their first gift in the first year. It does take time for individuals to trust you and your organisation and believe that you will make good use of their philanthropic gift. Each year you are building trust. The key reason for holding a £5,000 donor in your qualified caseload as described in Principle 4, is because they are capable of giving a higher level gift at a later stage if sufficiently motivated with the right project match.

A typical major gift executive, at the end of their first two years in the role, might have qualified approximately 30 people and be working towards perhaps qualifying a further 5 to 10. Once you have arrived at a caseload of around 30 to 40, it is time to **stop qualifying** and focus all your time on managing these important relationships. A key strategy for success is therefore to keep this qualified caseload small and manageable. Beyond this you are stretching your time capacity and will not be able to steward your caseload sufficiently.

In summary, to qualify 30 donors you need to start with three times that number of prospective major donors, working on an 'active' list of 30 to 40 at a time as described in Principle 12. If some fall away from your qualified caseload for various reasons such as their business fails and they can no longer give, you can, of course, look for new donors and prospects from the ranking list to replace them. However, one executive continued a relationship with a donor through the difficult financial time and eventually their business built up again and they were able to continue giving. This created an even stronger bond between this donor and the organisation.

I would suggest that, once a major gift executive has a full caseload of approximately 30 donors giving over £10,000 per annum, as an organisation you need to be looking to recruit the next major gift executive. The worst scenario is to put pressure on a major gift executive to manage more relationships.

However just to add in here that time can also be impacted by the types of programme supported. If all your qualified donors are supporting the same project (which is highly unlikely!) it may take less time than if 30 donors are supporting 30 different projects which require 30 sets of touch points. Whatever the scenario don't lose the overarching principle that financial success lies in a small and manageable caseload.

principle _____ 17

The successful executive decides when to use an introductory letter as the first contact

For some prospective major donors it may be appropriate to send an introductory letter by post or email to pave the way for the first phone call. There is a great debate on whether to use letters or not. Sending a letter is not a foolproof way of working as often the letter has not been read, however it can pave the way to give you confidence to telephone. Sending a letter is therefore most beneficial for the executive and is comforting as you build confidence in the area of prospecting. Once you gain confidence in making donor phone calls you will probably drop the use of a letter, but initially it can really help.

I remember one major gift executive who was struggling with making 'out of the blue' phone calls to donors even though they had given before. She then started the new strategy of sending letters first. It built her confidence and she achieved meetings when following up the letter with a telephone call. Some organisations go straight for the phone call, others send an introductory letter first. You can try both and decide which one works best for you.

The purpose of the letter is to prepare an individual for the phone call, thank them for their support, ask if the communication they receive is right, introduce yourself aligning yourself with the chief executive and in some cases, ask for their advice. Asking for advice regarding an up-and-coming campaign or a new work your organisation is thinking about developing can work well with very senior directors who are usually happy, if not flattered, to share their wisdom.

Here are three previously used, successful introductory letter examples:

1. *Dear Jonathan (If I may?),*

(Handwritten by you in blue pen, add 'if I may?', I learned this from the late Viscount Ingleby!)

I am writing to thank you once again for your generous support for the special project appeal last year for our work in Northumbria for Hannah and her community in Blacklocky.

(This assumes that he was thanked at the time. Add in any details here that are recorded such as any background, personal information known, latest gift size, event attended – whatever there is to make this letter personal for Jonathan Knight - to demonstrate that this not a direct mail piece!)

As you will know from the press reports, the project has been in desperate need of help from outside sources following the recent unprecedented storm in this area and North East Resource has played a key part in supporting families who lost their roofs.

My name is James Bennett and I am the Senior Relationship Executive at North East Resource. I work closely with our Chief Executive, Virginia Brown, and I was hoping to speak with you to introduce myself and provide you with feedback on how your giving has really helped the families in most need and to share some of the exciting work North East Resource is achieving. I would value hearing about your experience with NER as a regular supporter of this work and to receive assurance that you are receiving the right information.

Both Virginia and I recognise the vital role you play in making a difference in the North East and we are enormously grateful.

I would also value the opportunity to share with you highlights from NER's new strategic plan in lifting more families out of poverty.

If it is alright with you, may I give you a call next week? If you would prefer however, please feel free to be in touch using any of my contact details below. **OR** *We do not have a phone number or email address for you so perhaps you would be kind enough to phone or email me, and we can decide a time to speak to each other on the telephone at a time that is most convenient for you.*

(This last sentence is not ideal as they are not likely to contact you, however it is almost impossible to develop a relationship if

there is no telephone number; ideally study the research and locate a place of work and phone that number instead of using this sentence).

I am really looking forward to getting to know more about how I can be of assistance in the future and continue your relationship with North East Resource. You have given a huge amount of support in the last eleven years and I would like to find out what I can do to support you in return.

With very best wishes,

James Bennett
Senior Relationship Executive
(Don't use a title that implies fundraising, it is all about relationship first and seeking to match the potential donor's interests with the right proposal at a much later stage. For example don't use major gift executive – this is for internal use only!)

2.   *Dear Peter (if I may?),*

I hope that you don't mind me writing to you. Having recently joined North East Resource as part of the Relationships Team, working closely with Virginia Brown the Chief Executive, I very much wanted to write and introduce myself to you. I know that you have been a keen supporter of NER's development work in the past and thought that this was a wonderful opportunity to update you on some of the 'hot-off-the-press' strategic thinking as well as some of our more long-term achievements.

Last year NER benefited 400 people in 2 counties in the North East. This has been achieved through many gifts and generous donations from our supporters. We provided a response to 12 emergencies in 2 counties, including the crises caused by the recent storm in Northumbria. However, in evaluating and reflecting on some of our current development work, we have noticed a number of trends:

- *Poverty is getting more intense for excluded people in the North due to social and economic changes. NER will narrow its focus as a result of this.*
- *NER needs to focus more on building resilience of children to poverty.*
- *NER needs to be a greater advocate, addressing some of the causes of poverty in this locality to bring about significant change.*

We are also committed to seeing <u>real</u> change for families and our goal for the next five years is to see 1,600 families' lives transformed. An ambitious target but we are committed to seeing it fulfilled! Having just returned from the North East I can tell many stories of how this is working in practice. I'd love to share these with you!

I wonder how you would like to receive information about North East Resource, our new strategy and the impact that we are having with families living in poverty? As a key supporter of ours, it is my responsibility to ensure that you have sufficient information, as often as you require it and in the best format for you to digest.

I would love the opportunity to talk further with you about this and wonder if you would be happy to receive a phone call from me next week? If it is easier for you to communicate by email than telephone then please feel free to drop me an email at the address below.

I very much look forward to speaking to you in the near future,
With best wishes

James Bennett
Senior Relationship Executive

3. *Dear Sir Robert,*

    I hope that Lady Smithson and you are both keeping well.

    I am writing to thank you for your generous support of North East Resource's work over the years. My name is James Bennett and I am the Senior Relationships Executive for North East Resource. I work closely with our Chief Executive and Directorate Team, who all recognise the important role you play in making a difference in the North East communities.

    Have you ever pondered the fact that your joint patronage of NER's work spans 17 years in more than 3 counties! This is an outstanding achievement. Thank you, thank you and thank you again on behalf of the families and children whose lives you have changed.

    For your continual support of the North East work and your overwhelming response to the storm appeal for the Northumbrian families we are deeply grateful. You have put smiles on dozens of children's faces and made it possible for families to grow in these communities free of need and full of promise.

I was hoping to speak with you to introduce myself and hear about your experiences with North East Resource. If I may, I will give you a call in a few days. Please feel free to get in touch using any of my contact details below if you wish.

I look forward to speaking to you soon.

With very best wishes,

James Bennett
Senior Relationships Executive

These are three examples of friendly, introductory letters that could be used with a prospective major donor identified from your ranking list. They demonstrate different styles. You need to develop a letter that you feel comfortable using. There is no 'magic formula' letter, it just needs to be warm, friendly and personal for each individual demonstrating that you recognise the relationship the person has with your organisation. Simple!

Having sent the letter, before making the follow up telephone call, prepare yourself for the fact that your donor may not have read the letter or perhaps may have read it exercising skimmed reading and cannot remember what it said! So therefore have a verbal summary of the letter ready to give to the person you are calling.

Make absolutely sure that you keep accurate records of when you sent the letter and very importantly, meticulously telephone when you said you would. There have been many major gift executives who have sent out lots of letters to donors and not followed up. This is unacceptable. Unfortunately, the executive has perhaps phoned two to three times, not managed to make contact and given up. This can happen for many reasons:

Common Reasons for not following up	Action
Found the telephone number was not correct	Research and locate a work place telephone number and use this instead
Not found the individual at home during the day	Phone during the 6.00 – 8.00 evening slot; this is perfectly acceptable as charity is not 'work' to a donor, you are part of their leisure time; using the 6.00 – 8.00 slot should be a regular routine for the successful executive
No telephone number	Do not offer to call them in the letter – instead explain that you would like to have a conversation but do not have their number – ask if they could email or call you; it is unlikely they will but give them an opportunity **OR** if the letter is already sent, send a hand written note explaining as above. A donor without a telephone number (work or home) will be very hard to get hold of and you can only try email. If you don't have either focus first on donors where you do have the contact details

If a letter is sent and no contact is made after many attempts, it is good practice to send a hand written note to say you tried to contact them and would love to find out about their link with your organisation but have not been able to get hold of them and giving contact details for them to contact you. It is unlikely they will but you will have explained why you are no longer following up the letter. Close the relationship down. It is not good to have donors sitting within your 'active' list for weeks and months going nowhere. It is depressing for you and even more depressing for your manager! It is best to be decisive and round it off.

Note on your database all the actions taken, that the person was not spoken to, take them off your 'active' list and put them back in the main major donor pool. The person could well circle round again if they suddenly give a gift and that is definitely a better time to try again.

In summary, an introductory letter can help your confidence especially in the early days as an executive but is not essential. Many teams have dispensed with the letter and go straight for the phone call.

principle _____ 18

The successful executive prepares fully for the first phone call

The most successful opening to a first donor phone call is to begin with thanks. There is always something to be thankful for – the number of years they have supported, previous gifts, interest in your work or attendance at events. It is based on the information held on your database. Before making the call, read up and think through your opening story for each conversation.

At this early stage you are just aiming to build a rapport and your main goal is to secure a next contact, or 'touch point'. You need to be listening intensively during the call as to what that could be. It is your main purpose for the call. If you have a lovely conversation but no next action comes out of the call you are no further forward. Think on your feet as to what the next action could be as you listen to your donor.

It might potentially be to send any of the following - a two minute video, a link to a specific story on your website, succinct information on their interest, a photo, a biography of your new chief executive, the annual report, or whatever is appropriate for that person, gleaned from the call. Also remember that touch points need to be two way so let them know that you are interested in their feedback and opinions. You would therefore really like to know what they think of the information you send them.

All this needs to be conducted in a warm, friendly rather than intrusive manner. Most people do like to talk about themselves. If you are including a good mix of inquisitiveness about their interest in your organisation and some information the approach works well and will result in success with the next touch point secured.

The best case outcome from a donor or prospect phone call is to secure a first meeting. However, in our time poor world this is highly unlikely in the first phone call as trust has not had time to build, unless you are talking to a person who is already warm to your organisation and who knows a great deal about your work.

To prepare for the first phone call you need to have intentionality and give solid reasons, convincing reasons as to why you would like to meet the person. The more you rehearse these reasons the more confident you will be and the more likely the person is to respond. You can use a number of reasons for the meeting:

- To personally thank them for the years they have supported your cause
- To tell them more about a project they have previously given to
- To ask how they were first involved
- To ask if they receive the right amount of information
- To explain the new direction
- To describe the vision
- To ask their advice
- To introduce yourself
- To explain some changes that have taken place
- To demonstrate the link between the person and your organisation
- To explain the new strategic plan

It is also helpful to say that you work closely with the chief executive, of course checking that he or she is comfortable with the words you are using. As an executive you should be working closely with the chief executive and introducing him or her to key individuals you meet. This is one of many practical reasons why it is important to have your leadership committed to the programme. This also gives your donor confidence that they will be dealing with leadership at the highest level.

It is good to think ahead what you will say if the spouse or even a child answers the telephone. Some donors keep their interests and giving to themselves and therefore for privacy reasons it would not be appropriate to explain to the spouse why you are calling. However it is appropriate to give your name and the organisation's name and to ask when a good time is to call again without giving any details.

The most likely outcome of the first phone call with a person is not a secured meeting but rather your ability to move them to the next touch point which often is the emailing of more information for their preferred interest in your work. As the call progresses, you need to be actively listening and looking for what I call 'entry points' that lend themselves naturally to the next action point.

Preparation before the call is the key to success. Listening actively throughout the call to decide the most appropriate next touch point is crucial to success. Finally, the way to end the call successfully is to **agree** the next touch point with the donor while you are still on the telephone.

principle _____ 19

The successful executive sets up a report for notifications of donor actions

A very successful way of working is to immediately respond when a donor from your ranking list acts in some way with your organisation. The donor may send a gift, set up a direct debit or perhaps telephone reception and request information. Your donor is waving a hand saying 'I am interested' although, at this stage, it is up to you to discover how interested.

A notifications report is designed to let you know when any individual on your ranking list does something. You can receive these notifications of activity by setting up a weekly report from the flagged ranking list group on your database. Without this report you would rarely know these actions had taken place.

When a donor has just done something it is the best time to make contact. You will be able to immediately follow up with a phone call and begin the relationship. The notifications can include:

- Phone call to the office, an enquiry
- A donation, whatever size
- Request to join a specific segment, for example campaigning
- Attendance at an event

The report will notify you with a list of all actions by any person from the ranking list. Initially it is helpful to run a weekly database report of these actions. However, over time it may be possible to receive the report daily to enable a quicker response.

It is also good data management practice if you can encourage staff in supporter care to always ask the caller for their number if it is not logged on the database. It is not always possible as some calls are more of a confidential nature depending on the organisation but wherever possible they should ask the caller for their number. Other information that it is helpful to confirm is an email address, postal address and, in the UK, the donor's Gift Aid declaration.

Another form of notification can be carried out by eye by the staff member who processes donations in your organisation. If they are aware of private banking, they can alert you when they come across a cheque or payment detail of any size from a private bank. Donors who give donations with a premier current account are above-average earners or have a significant amount of money in savings or investments and tend to have more complex banking needs. Many of your prospective major donors will use private banking.

Once you have explained to staff why this information is needed, and they are open to assisting you, you hopefully will receive notifications in this way. It is an indication of the development of a philanthropy culture if the staff are willing to see themselves as part of the major gift process!

If the donor has just given, they are definitely a warm donor and it is the perfect time to telephone and thank them.

Below is a list of private banks in the UK and there may be others:

ABN AMRO Private Bank
ABC International Bank
ABSA Private Bank
ABSA Private Bank
Adam & Co Private Bank
Ahli United Bank
Allied Irish Private Banking
Arbuthnot Latham & Co
Bank of Scotland Private Client
Barclays Private Banking International
Brown, Shipley Private Banking
Butterfield Private Bank
C Hoare & Co
Cater Allen Bank
Child & Co Bankers

Citi Private Banking
Close Brothers Bank
Clydesdale Fleet Executive Banking
Coutts & Co
Dexia Private Bank
Emirates International
Fairbairn Private Banking
Habib Allied International
Halifax Private Banking
HSBC Private Clients
J P Morgan Private Banking
Julian Hodge Private Bank
Jyske Private Bank
Kleinwort Benson
Lloyds TSB Private Banking
NatWest Private Banking Direct
NatWest Private Banking Direct
Nedbank Private Bank
NM Rothschild & Son
Northern Bank - Premium
Royal Bank of Scotland Private Banking
UBS AG - Wealth Management
Yorkshire Bank Premium & Private

The report of notifications gives you an authentic reason for contacting the person. For example, to say thank you for the gift or direct debit (even though it's small) or to say thank you for attending a recent event or to ask if they received the information they requested. If you have their number, this conversation is always best by telephone as it builds the relationship much quicker than just sending an email. You can begin to get to know them and explore their interest in your organisation.

You need to take care how the notifications report is set up to avoid regular givers appearing on the report every month. It is really a database report for one off actions rather than regular gifts. The notifications report can accelerate your major gift programme providing you with a constant source of warm donors.

principle _____ 20

The successful executive listens 2/3 of the time and speaks 1/3 of the time

If there were only two lessons that I could teach about a major gift programme it would be firstly to focus on relationship building rather than aiming for finance and the second would be to use the following formula with every telephone call and meeting: listen 2/3 of the time and speak only 1/3 of the time.

It sounds very simple but is excruciatingly hard to implement and it has to be trained into your thinking to operate under this guideline. Your true test is to ask how much new information you have learned about the donor at the end of each phone call and meeting. You may have a bubbly personality, someone who likes to talk and who can pull an audience in to listen to the exciting things you are saying, however in major gift work you need to harness this and keep listening to your donor. Learning active listening skills can play dividends in this work.

I remember a time when I took a chief executive to see a wealthy cabinet minister. The appointment came up at the last minute and was an amazing opportunity to build a bridge with this significant individual. I watched him completely blow it as he talked the minister into the ground. It was painful. I could see the poor minister sinking deeper into his chair with discomfort, the chief executive completely oblivious talking away as this was his 'great opportunity'. Nothing was achieved and no further relationship built.

A way to train yourself to listen for 2/3 of the phone call or meeting is to prepare a comprehensive list of open questions and keep asking 'why' when offered responses. This is described in more detail in Principle 27. Develop a natural curiosity for information. Ask questions and aim to learn about the values and personal interests of your donor.

Think about these questions ahead of time and write down as many as you can. Have them in front of you ready to use at the appropriate times during the call. Here are some examples:

- Thanks for the donation or regular gift, is there anything that particularly prompted you to give this gift at this time?
- You've been involved with this charity now for 11 (?) years, thank you so much, how did you first become involved with this organisation?
- What aspect of our work most interests you? Prompt with examples
- Is there a particular area of the work that captures your enthusiasm?
- Any particular reason for that?
- Can I send you some succinct information? By e-mail? A video?
- What issues do you feel most passionate about?
- Do you come across these issues in your work?
- How did you find the Event? What was most interesting? What surprised you?
- Any aspect of our organisation's newsletter that you like best?
- Do you have children?
- What age are your children? (if appropriate connect with children supported in your charity)
- What's your experience with other charities? What charities are you interested in?
- How best can we serve you? Communicate with you?
- How best to stay in touch? E-mail? Phone? Text? Mobile?
- Can I meet with you and show you a short video of this aspect of our work?
- Would you like to visit our organisation? Meet our chief executive and directors?
- Are you willing to come on a journey with us to see our work in action?

Another list of questions is in Principle 27. You are unlikely to be successful at securing a meeting after the first call but your conversation, if you pursue active listening 2/3 of the time, should provide a great foundation for the next touch point and your future dialogue. This is a great step towards building a solid relationship.

Picture the Scene.......

Geoffrey telephoned a lady after she had sent in a gift of £250 to the charity. Her wealth band was showing her to be of considerable means, £10 million to £25 million. He talked long and hard about the charity, drowning out any answers to questions. He ended the call feeling very pleased with himself. The conversation led him nowhere. The information gleaned was zero.

Contrast this with:
Sophie telephoned a lady who sent in a £100 gift. She was shown to be in the £5 million to £10 million wealth band. Sophie asked lots of questions and discovered that the lady used to know the chief executive from 10 years ago; she had a personal connection with the organisation because her daughter had volunteered there just last year and had told her many good things about what they were doing. She was particularly interested in the programme for the elderly. Sophie was able to send her details of the new chief executive, and an outline plan of the new strategy for working with the elderly. She set up a further phone call for the following week.

Please don't be surprised if some people really do not want to know more and do not want a relationship with your organisation. You are not going to win everyone. Often the question 'What's your experience of other charities?' can reveal the answer. Your prospective major donor may well be fully engaged with another organisation, perhaps more than one, and not ready to carve out room for you in their busy schedule.

I remember a young trader who worked in the city and said

that we were about number 10 on his list of charities. We laughed about it as I asked him what we had to do to climb nearer to the top.

It is quite usual to engage only one person out of every three people that you speak to so don't let this deter you. You don't have to build a successful relationship with every individual. If you speak to three people and one responds well and you are able to move them closer to qualification to join your managed caseload, you are doing very well indeed!

The only successful way to be able to make this decision is to keep asking questions and ensure you listen for 2/3 of the conversation.

The final point is that you need to be truly authentic in your interest to find out the answers to these questions. As a major gift executive you need to be interested in people, interested in the lives of each of your prospective major donors, it is a vital part of your work. You cannot pay lip-service to this, genuine interest in each donor is the key to success and will bring the rewarding experience that any philanthropist is seeking from their relationship with a non-profit organisation.

principle_____21

The successful executive practises their first phone call until they are confident

Practice makes perfect. You will find that making first calls to prospective major donors will become easier the more you practise. Here are some tips for the telephone call

The Phone Call	Tips
1. Use both names if you have them "Is that John? John Brown?" rather than "is that Mr Brown?"	Aim to sound personal and not sound similar to a call centre – identify yourself quickly as from your charity – "this is Janet Brown from North East Resource....."
2. "Is this a good time to chat with you for a few minutes?"	Make it sound as if the call is going to be short and easy for them and gives them an 'out' if it is an inconvenient time

3. (If the donor is sounding harassed) "Can I call you back at a better time?"	If someone sounds busy recognise this. Don't prejudge and assume they aren't interested. It just may not be a great time for them. Offer specific alternative times for example tomorrow at 4.30 or 9.00, or at 1.00 on Friday until you find a good time. Stop yourself from assuming they are disinterested
4. Introduce yourself and your position	"I'm James Bennett and I work closely with our Chief Executive at North East Resource"
5. Use informal conversation as part of the introduction	Keep going until you can almost audibly hear the person relax, talk about the weather, their dog (barking in the background), the weekend, their village, their county......
6. Ask, "I just wondered, did you receive the letter I sent to you last week?" (if one is used)	They might not have opened the envelope and may not have read it so be ready for that

7. Explain again the reason for writing	Memorise the key points of the letter and summarise
8. Ask if it is alright to chat for a few moments	Have specific questions from your research ready for this conversation
9. Thanks for last gift, involvement, attendance at an event. If some time ago, say "Thank you *once again* for the gift sent in .... that was a great support towards..........."	Ask if there was anything in particular that prompted them at that time to give the gift? Even if it was 3 years ago they will often remember donating, have feedback ready if you know what project they gave to
10. Suggest that you would be really interested in hearing how they first became involved with your organisation	Ask questions, don't talk about yourself very much, you need to start probing motivations early in the relationship

11. Aim is not just to get them to talk but to engage with what they are saying and keep asking WHY?	For example: Wealthy individual: "I like x about your organisation ...." your response should be "oh that's interesting – why is that?" Rather than talking in great detail about the programme they like, ask why they liked it, your aim is to find out their interests
12. If there is a negative, don't answer it defensively, allow the supporter to have their say and "be heard"	Often all they need is the opportunity to get it off their chest. It is better to say "that's very interesting" "Oh I see" rather than jumping in too quickly to answer an objection
13. Get back to them with the answer quickly if you can't answer it in this call	Solid objections however need a solid response. Feel free to say "That's very interesting, if I may, I'll get back to you" if you don't know the answer and remember that objections are often reflections of interest

14. After the objection quickly get back to asking them questions about themselves again	Demonstrate 2/3 listening
15. "How familiar are you with all that we do?"	Practise a quick global description of your organisation often called the 'elevator pitch,' that is, you can explain it in the time it takes for a lift to get from the ground to the top floor
16. "Have you participated in any of our ....?"	Keep asking questions if you haven't found their motivation yet

17. Some business people want a bottom line answer as to why you are phoning them so be prepared	Rehearse (and rehearse!) an answer to this that you feel comfortable with such as: • I work closely with our chief executive and we are wanting to connect him/her with some of our key business contacts • We would like you to meet our directorate so we can get to know you and you us and will be holding small lunches to introduce you • We are looking to engage senior business people in our work and to ask for advice in all aspects of our work
18. "I would really like the opportunity to have a brief, 20 minute meeting. We are looking to involve high level individuals in our work. I would like to ask your advice on…….. Could we arrange a time?"	Be clear about defining the time. Sometimes they are not ready for this in a first call but have a next touch point in its place such as sending more information on the topic you have discussed

19. Have meeting times to suggest – offer three. "How about 28th September, 4th October or 8th October?"	Be directive and work a minimum of three weeks ahead, if they are very senior they will tell you when they can meet but still have three dates ready to offer to get the ball rolling. Don't feel tempted to use the "I am in your area on…….." unless they are in a remote area and this is applicable, better to say "I would like to come to Scotland, what date is good for you?" and then work other appointments around their date
20. Always finish the call with the next touch point in place.	Don't put the phone down without it. If you have forgotten, think of an excuse to phone them straight back and secure an agreed next touch point

21. Always ask for their email address by saying "Is it easier if I e-mail you the information?"	Find something that you need to e-mail to them based on your discussion, their answers and their motivation. You will get their email address more successfully than directly asking for it
22. Best case: Meeting arranged Or next touch point agreed. Worst case, not interested	If the person is not able to respond now, try "If it's alright with you, I'll contact you again after your conservatory is built, say in November" OR "If it's alright with you, I'll make sure you receive our Annual Report when it's published"
23. Don't let them finish the call by saying "I'll call you"	Truly they won't call you as you are not a priority for them at this stage of the relationship. If they do say "I'll call you" try "If it's alright with you, if I don't hear from you, can I call you at the end of September? I know how busy you are" They usually agree and you are back in the driving seat

I have found the phrase 'If it's alright with you………..' works very well. It softens what you are asking of them and gives the donor some control over the outcome. It is a great phrase to use frequently in these types of conversations.

It is difficult to achieve a meeting date during the first phone call however hard you have rehearsed, unless you have particularly good chemistry or they are very warm to your organisation. However don't be put off by this, if you are able to take them to the next touch point you have been successful. You will often find that after a few friendly touch points they are usually curious to meet you anyway!

The successful executive uses role-play to rehearse phone calls and meetings

It is good to practise role-play situations with peers. They are easy to make up and should be a regular exercise within your team. It is most effective to do this in three's if possible with one person acting as the observer, who can feed back immediately. If this is followed up with discussion on what went well and what not so well assessing the learning points from the exercise, it will help build your confidence. Here are some role-play examples:

Role-play 1: Mrs Judith Crawford

Mrs Crawford has been supporting North East Resource for fourteen years and always responds to appeals. She responded to the Northumbrian storm emergency and this was her first donation to an 'urgent' appeal. However she has recently had an issue with how much gift aid she has been paying and has had some communication with the Finance Team about this issue.

Mrs Crawford has never made a donation over £500 but you know that her wealth band suggests she might be worth £25million to £50million. Research has shown that her husband is an Investment banker in the city and she is involved in the local school governing board. You sent a new prospect letter to them last week and haven't been able to get hold of them until now. Judith answers the phone and you can hear ladies laughing in the background and cups of tea clattering around..........

Role-play 2: Peter Bernstein

Peter has recently given £4,000 through the website but up until now has never connected with North East Resource as far as you know. Your research has revealed that he is a Vice President of a large bank in London with a luxury apartment in Kensington. More in-depth research discovers that his daughter has recently gone to the North East on a gap year after studying at Exeter University. You also find out that he is someone who has typically received a huge bonus at the end of the tax year for the last four years and one article in The Guardian suggests that he wants to 'put something back' into society.

You emailed him to thank him for his gift and tried to arrange a phone call but you haven't heard anything back. You eventually find his work number on the bank website and decide to give it a go. After spending five minutes charming his personal assistant you are delighted she puts you through to Peter. You know that it's now June and you really want to wow Peter so he might at least consider NER when his bonus arrives next April.

'Hello, Peter Bernstein speaking..............'

You can also make up information about an individual and practise role-play to see if you can uncover this information from clever questioning. One of your team, acting as the donor knows the information but only reveals it if their role-play partner asks the right questions. Here are some examples:

Role-play 3:
Jeremy's wife has passed away. He has now remarried and has three children. His previous wife was extremely generous with finance. He always resented how much they gave away. After she died he realised what a blessing giving away finance had been and is determined to make up for lost time. His new wife is very supportive of giving and he has given at least three donations of £20,000+ to three different charities but cannot seem to find the right one that fulfils his interests in the North East where he visits regularly on business.

Role-play 4:
George stole money from a bank when he was in his 20's. He was charged and went to prison for 15 months. While he was in prison he made a determination to change his life. He is now 52. His current employers don't know he served time because he got the job in a merchant bank through friends. He is keen to not mention it. He feels that because he stole from society he should now put something back and give generously. He is giving to a charity but doesn't feel they are looking after him properly.

Role-play 5:

Heidi is an enthusiast of Scottish dancing and enjoyed this with her close friend Julia at St.Andrew's University. Julia decided to become a missionary and took the gospel and Scottish dancing to a tribe in Angola. The tribe became the only Scottish dancing tribe in Africa. Julia sadly died of malaria. Since then Heidi has wanted to support dancing tribes in Africa – particularly those that teach dance to their young. In fact she is keen to support any teaching of dance to the young particularly where she lives in the North East.

Role-play 6:

Michael and Joanne had difficulty conceiving and an even harder time adopting. After a long drawn out process they have an adopted daughter whose origins are from Senegal. Whilst they know their daughter is loved and cared for by them it has given them a heart for those living in poverty. They are quite new to this as they adopted their daughter when she was two and she is now five and it has taken them a while to get to this realisation. They are committed to providing support to her people group of origin but also to local families in poverty in the North East.

Role-play is a very effective way to build confidence and to become more alert to the possible directions a phone call or meeting can take. It offers practice in active listening and how to steer and influence the outcomes of the conversation. Although it can often feel awkward, it does enhance listening skills and is a practical application of the theory of finding out about the passions and interests of each donor.

principle 23

The successful executive learns how to overcome objections and build confidence with donors

Listening to objections is part of a major gift executive's daily life. The hard part is developing a positive attitude towards a donor's objections. It is helpful to remember that objections are often an expression of a genuine search for answers. They reflect your donor's attitude and values. In most cases, the donor is letting you know because they genuinely want the objection rectified.

In fact we want to encourage objections as they give us insight into the way the donor thinks and what is important to them. If he or she does not express objections you may not have communicated your charity's mission in enough detail. We want to encourage a discussion and hear their opinions, good or bad.

It is then that we can really bond with the donor and discuss our work with them. These judgments can take different forms and are a good sign that the donor is seriously trying to understand your work. He or she is looking through the window of their perceptions and sharing their world view and, as an executive, it is very helpful to hear this as you try to understand the donor. By doing this carefully and respectfully, you will go a long way to turn them from an adversary to a devotee.

The most important point is to remember that expressing an objection is not necessarily negative and to be successful, you should not perceive it as such. It can be an expression of interest.

The Confused Donor: This is to do with perceptions of the facts. Your donor may have differing perceptions to yours and the media can portray charities in a negative light. Your role is to clarify the information and give the donor the correct factual information - very gently!

The Indifferent Donor: This can often be worse than an outright objection. An indifferent person is showing no interest in your organisation and you have little to work with. A way through this is to summarise what they have said and then ask more questions to try and clarify their interest. As some have said 'the opposite of love is not hate, rather it is indifference.'

The Sceptical Donor: Often this is a reflection of a donor's experience. This experience may differ to what you are presenting. A way round this is to include an expert, a programme person from your staff or a trustee, who can share facts, observations and experience of your work to bring confidence where the donor is communicating scepticism.

A Specific Objection: A specific objection is often wrapped in strongly felt emotions and is often based on a donor's life journey. It is hard to neutralise by argument or even facts. They need to be acknowledged and sensitively worked through. There are no short cuts. It may take time but it is always worth it. They are a genuine demonstration of interest. The donor is often looking to you to have an answer. The way to do this is to clarify to show you understand. Re-state the objection as a question. Ask more questions to narrow it down and then bring it into the bigger picture. Emphasise all the good that is being achieved. Often an individual will feel happier once their objection has been declared and they have felt 'heard'. Sometimes this is all it takes. It is a question of scale. A specific objection about how your organisation operates may require a meeting with leadership and cannot be answered sufficiently by you alone.

It is a useful exercise to notate every possible objection that you can think of and prepare possible answers. Here are some examples:

"Why are you phoning me? You must be busy – why waste your time?"
- "I am phoning to say a more personal thank you"
- "We have decided to talk to some of our closest supporters and find out what special interests they have"
- "I am phoning because you are an amazing supporter and I really don't want you to think that we take that for granted it's fantastic what you do and have done in the past"
- Use their name if deemed appropriate "the last thing I want to do Jonathan is something that you don't feel comfortable with......."
- "We thought it would be helpful if you had the opportunity to put your gift to something specific where you and your family can see how your gift has changed lives.........."
- "We just want you to have a really good experience with us", move to a question "What has been your best experience with a charity?"

"I can see how lives are changed through stories and get all the information I need on the website or in resources anyway...."
- "The information I would provide will be a lot more personal for you, that is, demonstrating what your gift has done specifically"
- "The website isn't updated as often as the information I have, also much of the detail cannot be there because of space; it is designed for quick reading"
- "It could be more meaningful for you if you were able to give to a work that you have some connection with. We are keen for you to hear about projects that matter to you and your family"
- "Perhaps together, once you know more about our work, we can work out where the match is........."

"I am happy with the money to go to where the need is greatest"
This can almost sound indifferent. We want the donor to give to a specific project or programme so that it is easier to feedback the results. Without this it is much more difficult to come up with relevant monthly touch points.

- "That's great. I am wondering if it would be more meaningful for you to see actual beneficiaries lives changed because of giving to a specific project that your family believe in and can relate to"
- "Giving to a specific project will also connect you with a specific part of our work and the needs"

"Your charity sends out too many mailings"
- "I am sorry if it seems too much for you, obviously our heart is that we are keen to let people know about our work and the needs"
- "I would be delighted to organise things for you so that you only receive what is helpful to you"
- "What would you prefer to receive? How often? Would you prefer it by e-mail?"

Note - don't mention 'our system' – we don't want them to think they are just a name on the database, for example "On our system it says to send you all mailings…"

"How is the recession hitting your organisation? Is your income down?"
- Prepare an answer from the Annual Report, comments from the Chairman or from your Finance Director

The key point to remember is that handling objections are part of your work. They are to be embraced, welcomed and gently worked through. Your donor will be more supportive of your cause once their objections have been heard and answered! A relationship is often stronger if the objection is faced head on and answered to the prospective major donor's satisfaction. They will appreciate the time you have taken to listen and convince them. It is worth taking that time and using it to build a deeper relationship.

principle _____ 24

The successful executive uses the phone tirelessly

Using the telephone is one of the most important aspects of the job of a major gift executive. Yet I have observed that executives often hesitate and sometimes over think each call. All of us struggle to make calls to people we don't know so don't be surprised if this is you. Prospecting to find the right major donors to qualify on to your caseload is not easy. Realise that the reason for the call must be based around providing the donor with more information, insight and a better, more rewarding service which they will find of value.

The best advice is to realise that thinking about the call can actually be more stressful than making it! There could be good reason for your inhibition to making calls:

- Your desk is quite public and other staff can hear what you are saying; this is particularly embarrassing if you are working on donor calls where you have no idea how the prospective major donor is going to respond
- You are prejudging when the best time is to call; you are thinking more about when to call than actually calling
- You have not owned the fact that the call is about the donor, not you
- You haven't fully realised that prospecting is about opening relationships and you won't be able to build any if you haven't made the phone calls
- You haven't fully thought through the fact that this is a blessing for the donor and your call will radically improve their day!

If necessary, find other places to call, even using your mobile in your car! Don't over think it and just get on with the job. Realise this is about the donor and offering them a great experience with your organisation. Focus on their feelings rather than your own. Know that the telephone is the main way to begin the journey and use it often! Honestly, don't over think it, just do it! Success breeds success and once you have experienced some great telephone calls you will be inspired to do many more.

Once you have prepared the background notes on your 'active' list of donors and noted the key questions to ask, keep those notes handy and keep calling at all different times of day and evening until you get through. Use call barring so they do not see evidence of the same number calling them. Phone as many of your donors as possible in one sitting. You will definitely get through to some. It is often to do with numbers.

One executive I know uses the phone tirelessly. He knows it is all about numbers. He can phone up to 150 donors in one sitting. He says that statistically he has to be able to get through to some. He enjoys it and has some lovely conversations and because he is so used to phoning he is totally relaxed and his donors can sense that too. He has something of value that he wants to share. He also knows that if he doesn't believe in himself and speak with confidence and energy his donors won't pay attention to him.

I am not suggesting that you should keep 150 active donors ready to call as 30 to 40 is more focused, however there is a lesson here of not being afraid to call and just getting on with the job.

Because some find this so difficult you might consider recruiting a 'hunting' executive for prospecting who loves the chase, someone who is persistent and willing to phone tirelessly. This type of individual is superb at courting interest from donors and prospects and securing a first meeting. A salesman will love this first part of relationship building, however the nurturers of relationships will find it difficult. So consider this very carefully when recruiting as described in more detail in Principle 5.

On balance the phone is underused by most of the executives I have trained and worked with. I think this is mostly because there is a great fear of saying the wrong thing and perhaps 'blowing it' at the first point of contact. If you feel the phone is intrusive, try and get over it as it is the lifeblood of your work as a major gift executive. Aim to make at least three phone calls to donors on your 'active' list or to your qualified caseload donors every day. Once you have enjoyed success in your calls, you will begin to see the results of building a qualified caseload of warm relationships. If you keep phoning, you will definitely get there.

If you have a choice of post, email or telephone always choose the telephone as your first option. It builds the relationship quicker. However, each donor will have their preferred way of communicating. Some prefer email and not the telephone, others never respond to emails but will quite happily chat when you ring them and this may be the only way to get their attention. Remind yourself you are not their top priority but over time your organisation will become more important to them as they get to know you.

A good tip when phoning a donor at the office is to call just before the hour. Most meetings start on the hour which means the one time you might be able to catch the person is just before a meeting starts. Often for the first call, the important part is actually speaking to the person. You can always rearrange a better time to talk during the call.

Prospecting is hard work. However it can be richly rewarding as you slowly build your qualified caseload. The important part for you is to keep phoning tirelessly. It is the only way to be successful and progress quickly.

principle _____ 25

The successful executive doesn't use the phrase 'I am in your area on.....'

Does saying to a donor 'I would like to meet as I am in your area' really work? I would venture to say 'No it doesn't work!' Yet it is used frequently by executives. Here are some reasons why I don't think it is appropriate.

Firstly it can appear arrogant. It is conveying the impression that 'I, the major gift executive, want to see you when I think it is convenient and when I don't have to go out of my way'. Therefore the underpinning value could be perceived as 'My time is more important than yours.'

Secondly it often stems from fear. The executive is trying to appear nonchalant and apologetic when really they perhaps lack the boldness and courage to say 'I want to meet with you because you are important to this work, important to us and I am interested in your views on.....' whilst also thinking 'and therefore you are worthy of all the time it will take me to drive to your house or office', which is a much more positive underpinning value.

Thirdly, it can appear that the donor is second best to another appointment the executive already has scheduled for that day. This is not good on a number of fronts and may portray to the donor that they are just a number, one of many, or worse they are second in the diary rather than first on that day and the executive needs to fill in the time.

A goal for an executive is to make every donor seem special and to communicate how much you are going out of your way just for them. Prospective major donors desire a high level of service and attention, so you need to give it to them. They are individuals and need to be thought about individually. When working with executives, I always say it is alright to do only one appointment in a day. It is far better to do this than to procrastinate meetings until another person has agreed to a visit nearby on the same day.

Trust is something we want to build with each major donor so it is perhaps not appropriate to make up 'I will be in your area on....'.
I would therefore suggest you don't say it and go for boldness instead. Put potential dates in the diary of when you would like to go and offer one. No need to use the hesitant 'I am in your area on....'.

Also practise and practise the reasons why you want to meet with them. Many donors admire boldness and truthfulness. This is not about wanting a large gift but rather 'thank you for your interest, your gifts have made a difference...'. Also try 'I work closely with our chief executive and she is keen to meet senior level individuals....' or 'I would very much like the opportunity to explain our global strategy that will greatly enhance the service to the beneficiaries we serve'. To achieve a meeting date on the phone call I would have ready three potential dates in the diary to offer as described in Principle 21.

I remember a donor in Northern Ireland who always said 'only come and see me if you are in Northern Ireland, but don't come specially'. An executive decided they were fed up with this and said 'I want to come and see you, you are important to us and I'm coming'. The donor agreed and eventually this resulted in a £60,000 gift.

However, some donors may offer the objection that they don't want you to spend your time visiting and definitely don't want you to drive to their area especially to see them. Often this can be false modesty so push back a little bit and try 'of course I would like to meet you... if you are busy let's stick to one hour' or adjust this to 20 minutes if visiting them in a fast paced office, 'I would be delighted to meet you, you're important to us'. For the occasional few who really mean it and only want you to come when you have an appointment nearby, of course comply with their wishes.

However, I would suggest using this ONLY when it is appropriate and ONLY to answer the objection of not wasting your time travelling to visit only one person.

The main message here is to speak with passion and be confident and bold at explaining why you want to meet them. High level individuals respect this. Why would they want to meet you if you sound hesitant? It won't work with everyone but then as a successful executive you don't want everyone, only the donors that respond to you and want to engage more.

principle _____ 26

The successful executive meticulously plans their first donor meeting

The key objective of the first meeting is to make a decision as to whether to qualify this person or not on to your caseload. If the meeting has been arranged three weeks in advance, do take the time to send a confirmation email regarding the date, time and place for the meeting.

If you are meeting in a hotel or café it is lovely if the donor offers to pay (and often they do) but don't worry about buying a nice lunch or afternoon tea for you and the donor. Your manager should understand the need for this investment.

As you prepare for this first meeting, read the research from your prospect researcher or from a company produced profile. Make sure you have looked them up on the internet and have established some facts about them. You will also have tracked any relationship they might have with your organisation from your database. This could range from 'sent a £50 donation' five years ago, attended an event, sponsors a child, has a connection with a trustee' to 'on our database and receives newsletters'.

This information gives you a platform on which to begin the conversation, thanking them for giving, attending, sponsoring, and receiving your newsletter. Always start with thanks and, if they have given a gift, some feedback on the work the donor has supported in the past. They were clearly motivated to give at that time and it is a great place to start the conversation. Perhaps show them a 2 minute video or some prepared pictures of the work and its success.

During this opening focus on the beneficiaries and how the work has helped those in most need. Demonstrate something of the difference the donor has made for giving the gift to the project, even if it was only a small gift. You want to instil the joy of giving and encourage this to be a great experience for your donor.

The most important point to remember in this first meeting is that you should use the opportunity to listen. You need to be alert to recognise the person's values and to dig deep to find out what really interests and motivates them. If you do most of the talking during the meeting, what have you learned to write down on the post meeting contact form? So follow the 2/3 listening, 1/3 speaking rule and you will have much to record on the donor's interests and motivations as described in Principle 20.

Prepare yourself fully to be ready to answer any of the following typical philanthropist questions, any of which could arise in your first meeting:

- What motivates your employees and staff?
- What will the organisation look like in 5 years? 10 years?
- What are your current costs per client?
- What sort of impact are you getting for that?
- Summarise your current strategic plan for me
- Who is doing similar work?
- How are you working with, or at least learning from them?
- What sort of professional training do your staff have?
- What is your £ turnover? Is it increasing each year?
- How does the organisation define success?
- Are you reaching it?

Prepare a short, succinct verbal description of your charity, its mission and key facts that you estimate may interest your potential donor and practise being exciting and fluent at explaining this. Study the research beforehand and make a good guess as to what they *may* potentially be interested in. You are looking for what I call 'entry points' or 'hooks'. If you know a possible match of interest such as their business takes them to Bolivia and your charity works in Bolivia, focus on this. Perhaps show them a one minute video on your tablet or laptop of the work your charity is doing in Bolivia.

Throughout the meeting you should be the one asking the

questions as this keeps you in the driving seat. You need to be the one driving the conversation so that you achieve your goal of finding out as much as you can about the donor and deciding what the next touch point should be following this meeting. Ask leading questions in this first meeting as described in Principle 20.

Remember they are asking: Am I convinced by what they are telling me? Are they trustworthy? Are they really committed to their charity or is this just a job for them? Do I want to pursue this? Do I like this person? Are they sticking to the time agreed? The longer you do the talking the more time you are giving them to be asking themselves these questions. If you allow them to talk, they will enjoy the meeting more and will feel a valued participant rather than being 'spoken at'. It is a fact that people remember what they have told you not the other way round. So resist the temptation to talk too much. Exercise the 1/3 speaking 2/3 listening rule. This is particularly important in the first meeting.

Speak for a short time, only a couple of minutes, and then ask a question to engage the person in what you have just said. This doesn't always come naturally so practise this ahead of time. It feels far more natural to keep talking but refrain from doing this as it can quickly become too much information and you are in danger of boring the person. Try to be cautious about talking about yourself and personal information unless the person asks. It is a balance. However in some cases this can be helpful. Highly skilled major gift executive Mary Smith, Associate Director of Leadership Giving, Habitat for Humanity International, on this subject said:

"In showing my vulnerability it can give the donor permission and courage to also make themselves vulnerable. From feedback I have had from donors it is when I have been very personal, passionate and emotive that it has had an impact on them. For example, when I spoke about the refugees I met in Lebanon whilst working for World Vision. When talking about philanthropic and personal values I think it does become a very personal conversation and it's hard to achieve if you as the executive have to remain in 'professional' mode. It's certainly a delicate balance but if you don't give anything of yourself away then I think you will not achieve the full depth of conversation that you want".

It can be quite difficult tipping a conversation from professional to personal but generally speaking, be brief and get focused back on them again and keep asking questions.

If you asked for a 20 minute meeting, be sure to watch the clock and at the end of 20 minutes remind them that the time is up. They have a choice then to either ask you to stay longer or round up the meeting. By giving them the option you have respected their time and in a natural way have built trust even at this early stage of the relationship. They can be assured that you keep your word.

Have the next touch point ready to suggest at the close of the meeting. During the meeting you can assess what that should be. It might be:

- Email them a summary of some information that has come up during your meeting
- Email them a link to a video
- Agree to phone them next week to hear their reaction to some information you are leaving with them
- Invite them to visit your office
- Organise a meeting with your chief executive or a trustee
- Offer a meeting with a particular programme manager related to their interest
- Agree to meet their spouse as well

Do not leave the meeting without the next touch point in place, otherwise you will not know what to do next. The time to agree with them what the next step should be, is in your meeting. They are likely to stick to it as you have agreed this next step together.

The most successful major gift executives have learned how to do this skilfully. The role of the executive is to a degree, one of sales demonstrating your passion for your organisation's mission, but it is mainly one of active listener with detailed attention to observing and understanding how the donor is reacting to you and from that observation naturally flowing into the next touch point.

principle _____ 27

The successful executive keeps asking 'why'? A practical example

During every meeting use the question 'why?' continuously as this encourages the person to reveal some deeper aspects of their interest. If they suddenly say 'Oh that's really interesting...' don't use it as your cue to talk a lot, rather turn it back to them and ask 'oh really, why is that of particular interest to you?' If you keep asking 'why', you will find out a lot about the person. Here is a practical example to bring this to life:

You are visiting Harry Braithwaite for the first time. In this first meeting you are keen to learn as much as you can about Harry to decide if he is interested enough in your work for you to qualify him on to your caseload. You therefore need to listen actively to every signal given and every word that Harry says. Implicit in this is that you ask questions and don't talk too much. In the first meeting, it is important to enthuse about your mission and be convincing, but keep reversing back from speaking and ask questions, carefully listening to the responses using the speak for 1/3 and listen for 2/3 rule.

Harry: *"So, your organisation responds to overseas emergencies – what is happening right now?"*

You could easily use this as your cue to talk enthusiastically to answer his question about what your organisation is doing admirably for the emergency. Yes this is good and great to answer Harry's question however, exercise self control and, after two – three minutes, focus on Harry by perhaps saying *'It is great that you are asking me, do you have a particular interest in emergencies? Why is that?'* Be prepared that some people may not have answers to these deep questions, but you are encouraging Harry to think more deeply about his interests even if it takes him a few minutes to formulate his views.

The key point is that if you ask Harry questions, he will answer. If you don't ask enough questions, the meeting will be over and you haven't learned any more about Harry's passions, interests and more importantly will not be equipped enough with the knowledge of how to continue the relationship flow. Also remember that people love talking about themselves. I read years ago that people mostly remember what they have said to you and not what you have said to them and I have never forgotten that! So Harry's positive memory of the conversation will be about what he said to you.

Therefore, ask lots of questions: Do you have family? Do you have to commute far into work? Do you play golf? (any clues in his office as you look around?) You can tactfully and gradually learn a lot about Harry. This is so crucial to your future philanthropic relationship. Before going to the meeting make a long list of potential questions to ask Harry as described in Principle 20 and memorise them and use your skills of discernment to assess which questions will be most suitable in the meeting.

Watch his reaction. Is he leaning forward, or sitting back in the chair? Are his eyes darting around or are they focused on you? Is he responding to what you are saying by nodding or asking questions? Is his body language open? You need to be genuinely interested in Harry and his life, his loves and hates, his hobbies, his work, his children, his pets, his interests and his music. If you are not then you will struggle with this job. Liking people, being genuine and wanting to go on a journey with them at their pace is critical to being a successful executive. It requires patience.

Before leaving the appointment, determine what the next point of contact or touch point will be. If you have listened well there will be lots of potential touch points for you to suggest. There is therefore a natural flow to the relationship:

'Thanks so much Harry for our conversation today. I'll send you through those photos and would be really interested in your feedback ……… I'll give you a call ……….. oh and would love to meet your wife ………..also to hear how your dog got on at the vet………..'

Immediately after the meeting write down the key points that Harry said and keep track of what you have learned so far. Many organisations use 'Donor Contact Forms' or keep the information on their database. Write it down straight away as the longer the gap of time the less you remember. I always recommend it should be within 1 – 2 hours after the meeting.

It will often take at least 9 months of relationship building before donors like Harry are ready to consider making a significant gift and be 'asked' to give to a project that matches their interest. For some it could take 12 to 18 months or more depending on the individual. Every prospective major donor is different and this is what keeps you on your toes! Not every person will be interested in your mission. Find the ones that are, qualify them on to your caseload and work with them. The important part is a natural relationship flow.

Finally, enjoy yourself. Giving is a very positive act. Wealthy individuals enjoy hearing about the difference they have made and thrive on the satisfaction it brings. To be a successful executive, be intentional about the relationship and where you are taking them. The only way to navigate this journey with your major donor is to ask questions, keep asking why, listen carefully to the answers and respond with the right plan.

principle _____ 28

The successful executive keeps the contact flowing naturally

Executives sometimes ask me how often they should contact their prospective major donor during the relationship building, cultivation phase. There is no hesitation in my answer to this question – it is a minimum of monthly. If you have had no contact with a donor for over a month, he or she has already moved on to other things. It is therefore vital to keep the relationship flow going at least monthly.

Of course, this is never discussed with your donor. You could not say 'Can we stay in touch monthly?' as any normal person would reply 'What! I'm far too busy for that'. Rather it is a natural weaving of touch points, back and forth as the relationship develops. It could be as simple as short texts, a meeting or phone call, sharing beneficiary stories, meeting a director or whatever is natural for that particular person and your relationship with them.

However, it does need to be meaningful with the aim of continually deepening the donor's understanding of your work whilst maintaining a growing friendship. It must have purpose, be mutually beneficial, and will eventually result in your donor engaging with a particular aspect of your work and joyfully giving a philanthropic gift.

Although this is an altruistic aim, it has to be grounded practically and monthly contact is a must. A helpful hint is not to leave contact until your next arranged meeting date. It is tempting to think 'whew – I don't need to do anything with this person until next month's meeting'. It should be a constant flow. If you have booked a meeting in a month's time don't feel tempted to just leave it at that. You will have sent an email to confirm the time and date of the meeting but you can do so much more than this. Continue the flow of conversation. You could ask questions about the meeting, what to bring, what videos they would be most interested in, depending on their interests.

Lots of interaction is the most effective way to deepen the relationship. Think about the conversation you had on the phone, the subjects discussed. You should be able to keep the flow of contact going before the meeting and not wait for a month by which time the relationship could start to cool. For example an email might read:

Dear Jonathan,

It was great talking with you on Friday and once again thank you for the interest and passion you have demonstrated for supporting families in poverty in the North East. As we were talking on the phone you asked about the specific work that had been done following the devastating effects of the highly unusual storm in the North East of England.

Although we will talk more about this when we meet, I have just received the latest information regarding the families who were most affected from our programme coordinator. Please see below for the latest update on this situation.

(Insert a paragraph or two of news..................)

I trust you find this very encouraging.

I look forward to seeing you on the 24th at 2.00 p.m. and sharing an outline of our long term plans for the North East. It will be exciting to briefly take you through them. If you have any questions in the meantime, please let me know.

On another note, how is your daughter settling in at Exeter University? Did you manage to get everything in the car?? (Smile)
Best wishes,
James

In the example above Jonathan may not answer the email but he may have glanced at it, so that is therefore another step in relationship building. The newer the relationship, the less likely people will respond but as the relationship warms the person will begin to enjoy your company. Publications from The Centre for

Philanthropy, University of Kent, reveal that one of the most enjoyable aspects for philanthropists is their relationship with the non-profits they support.

Another hint is to always end an email with a question. The question should be specific as in the above example, *'Did you get everything in the car?'* rather than general *'Is there anything else you would like to know?'* This makes it much easier for the person to respond and you want to encourage them to engage with you as much as possible!

If they are a 'phone' or 'text' person then give them a quick ring or text to say, for example, *'just received the latest news from the North East – I've sent you a short email. Hope it encourages you'*.

Philanthropists are time poor but they do want to know about the causes they support. It is only as you get to know a person that you can find the right way to do this. You may feel worried about overdoing the contact, and some people may not want much information or indeed any contact which is why it is so important to qualify only those who do want to hear more from you. The key is finding a way to naturally move the relationship forward through a series of relevant touch points.

I have seen executives have a sprawling list of donors who they contact every now and again. This is not the best way to secure mutually beneficial relationships. Limit the number you are trying to make contact with and keep contact with them until you are in a position to decide whether they will form part of your qualified caseload or not. Don't be afraid to let them go. It is likely that you will only qualify one in three anyway so two out of the three will go back to the major donor pool as described more fully in Principle 16.

Successful prospecting is about having the stamina to keep the relationship going in a way that is richly rewarding for the donor, but also having the confidence to know when to let them go. It is about being creative in your questioning and listening to his or her preferred way of working and fulfilling their need to make a difference in the world. Monthly touch points are not about 'bothering' a busy person, but rather offering a transformational experience for each donor. A successful executive truly understands the donor's joy in giving.

principle _____ 29

The successful executive's check list for prospecting

I am using the term 'prospecting' here to mean converting a wealthy donor, who may have given a gift to your work in the past, into a qualified prospective major donor, who will eventually give a major gift to your cause, well in excess of £10,000.

Here is a summary of the key points for prospecting, a check list for the successful major gift executive:

- Make your introductory letter (if used) mostly about the donor – not all about you or your organisation
- Align yourself with your chief executive in your letter and on the telephone
- Don't send out more prospective major donor letters if you haven't followed up the previous ones
- Use your research to prepare your opening story of why you are contacting them
- Always start with thanks as part of the story
- Be excited and determined when contacting donors
- Make the phone your best friend
- On the telephone, if the donor sounds busy, re-arrange another specific time to talk
- Although a meeting is the best case result for a phone call this may not be achievable so secure a next touch point instead – eventually they will want to meet you
- Prepare a long list of questions before each phone call and before each meeting
- Don't be in a position where you kick yourself afterwards for not asking a key question

- Rehearse what you are going to say using role-play
- Have your elevator pitch rehearsed and ready
- Keep abridged of the organisational strategic plan and be able to explain it in under three minutes
- Listen for 'entry points' – demonstration of warmth, questions, positive comments, good body language from your donor and build on these
- Make it your goal to learn about the donor's interests and passions
- Keep asking 'why'?
- Use the phrase 'if it's alright with you' often
- Learn to embrace objections and view them as a genuine expression of interest
- Respond to what people tell you
- Offer a first class service – be quick to respond to their need
- Accept a no – if they are not interested they are not interested
- But also don't give up easily
- Stay in touch monthly with each donor – anything less and they are lapsing
- Above all – LISTEN for 2/3's of the meeting or phone call and meet them where they are – it is a skill that can be learned – only talk for 1/3 of the conversation
- Introduce each donor to your organisation's directors
- Write down everything your donor said within 1 to 2 hours of the meeting
- Limit the number of donors you work with
- Contact at least three donors each and every day

principle_____30

The successful executive writes the twelve month plan early in the relationship

At the first meeting with your donor you may be able to make the decision to qualify the person. See Principle 15. If this is the case, during the meeting you need to be thinking about the potential twelve month plan for this newly qualified person. It is crucial to find out all you can while you are with them, even in this first meeting. Keep asking questions and include 'why' after they have given you an answer as described in Principle 27. This will drive you deeper into understanding their motivations.

After qualifying the donor on to your caseload, it is essential that with some urgency, you write the plan for them for the next twelve months including an estimate of the most appropriate time for the donor's 'ask'. The sooner you write the plan the sooner you will have a sense of direction and the more successful you will be in developing the relationship. The plan gives you intentionality about the direction of the relationship.

Below are some simple examples of information that could be gleaned in the first meeting if you have followed the active listening 2/3 and speaking 1/3 rule and are alert to asking key questions. This vital information can be used in your twelve month plan.

Some of this information is discerned by you from the answers given. Here are some examples:

Questions asked to glean information	Information learned from questions	Ideas of how to use this information in the twelve month plan
How did you hear about our organisation in the first instance? When did you first ask to receive our information? Why did you give your first gift?	Owns so much and wants to give back to society	Definitely has a good propensity for giving, aim high in the 'ask' on the plan, 'ask' sooner than you originally thought – assuming right project identified
Are you involved with other charities? Which ones? In what way?	Feels disorganised in giving, has no specific relationship with one organisation	Explain different methods for giving, align them to a specific project that interests them, include how meaningful it can be to fund the specific project and see the results with videos, regular short reports, meetings with project leader
Are your family involved in the organisations you support? How would you like to engage them? How can you achieve this?	Wants to include the family in the decision and see the difference made to beneficiaries	Include the children in your plan, take giveaways for the children to meetings and specific child friendly beneficiary stories

Do you travel with your job?	Travels to East Africa and Portugal in global portfolio (this also could be a city in the UK)	Describe a project linked to that area to gain interest
Do you have children? How does that make you feel about other children who aren't as well off?	Wants to help children	Include child centred projects and videos on your plan
What first attracted you to this organisation? Why was that? Which aspect of the work intrigues you the most? When succinctly describing your charity give specific examples of the work, one at a time, and follow clues to their interest such as body language and questions asked	Interested in a particular aspect of your work – specify which project	Make the plan all about their specific interest although remembering that prospective major donors also like to know the strategy and vision for the organisation as well as detail about the specific project

Try not to conduct the meeting like a formal interview. You are building a friendship and want to respond warmly to what the person is telling you. This is not a business meeting. The ability to listen and watch body language and know when to speak more and when to hold back is part of the art of a successful major gift fundraiser.

When you leave the meeting write down everything they said to you in answer to your questions on your laptop or tablet. Do this quickly within 1 to 2 hours of the meeting, after that you will begin to forget some of the detail. This information is really important and forms the bedrock of your future plan. What to include in the twelve month plan is described more fully in Principle 31.

The fundamental elements of what you are trying to achieve in the twelve month plan is to help the prospective major donor to:

- Understand the vision and strategy of your organisation together with its values
- Have a deep, healthy relationship with you, the major gift executive, the directors and the programme staff (important it is not just you)
- Receive information relevant for their specific project interest and passion for the work
- Be communicated with in the right way for them (phone, email, texts, regular meetings)
- Be presented with a financial need and asked for financial support (at the right level, a minimum of £10,000)
- Receive thanks and reports that specifically tell them what their investment did in personal and measurable terms
- Increase or maintain their giving each and every year

The successful executive prepares the twelve month plan on a relationship chart for each qualified donor

A strategy is simply your plan to get you where you want to go. It is crucial to have a twelve month plan, your strategy, for each **qualified** donor outlining what action you will take each month throughout the coming year. For some this may need to be a twelve to eighteen month plan. Without a plan you are shooting from the hip, working randomly and will move the relationship forward haphazardly.

This doesn't mean that you don't encourage the donor to have the freedom to determine the way they want to work with you and your organisation. Philanthropists have needs they want to have met and values they want to express. You must listen and help them fulfil these goals. But as a major gift executive, you need to stay one step ahead and this requires a strategy.

At the start of the planning process, your first step is to plan when the 'ask' will be for the simple reason that more preparation and follow up time is needed before and after the 'ask'. It might require coordination with other teams or members of staff to allow time for a team to develop a proposal or to get time in the chief executive's diary. If you have 30 to 40 prospective major donors on your caseload you need to plan the 'asks' in order to space them out throughout the year so as not to have too many 'asks' in one month. You also have to do this in line with the donor's desired time to give, which is unknown in the early stage of the relationship.

Therefore at first the 'ask' is placed in a month starting with a best guess, but as you get to know the person, you can adjust the 'ask' to be more accurately placed. In theory the earliest time for an 'ask' would be once you have completed a minimum of 9 months of touch points. However, you make the judgment of when the 'ask' should be, as some may be enthusiastic and ready to give sooner, others might take longer. You are the judge as you are the only person who knows them well.

Add donor visits to your plan as often as they will allow because a face-to-face meeting is always the most effective relationship touch point.

Also bear in mind that donors who work in some industries in the City will get an end of year bonus and so timing 'asks' to meet the tax year end can be beneficial.

The plan for each donor should weave naturally and seamlessly through the months of the year towards the 'ask' and should continue monthly with thank you's and stewardship demonstrating the difference the donor has made after the gift is given.

A simple relationship chart spreadsheet can provide the tool for planning. Some teams incorporate the equivalent of a monthly planning spreadsheet directly on to their contact database. It is impractical to include a relationship chart example here but if you email me at ruth@ascentphilanthropy.co.uk I will forward an example to you.

Although this might seem prescriptive in fact the opposite is true. It is very freeing. If you are in the middle of a very busy job maintaining contact with donors every day, the relationship chart offers you an instant 'to do' list of all the people you need to contact before the end of each month describing what you need to do and helps with prioritising and time management.

It is really important to maintain this flow of touch points with your qualified donor writing them succinctly on your chart, a few words reminding you of the subject. These should be personal such as 'ask about dog' or 'conservatory' or 'daughter – Exeter University' as appropriate and will most importantly include relevant information about your organisation such as 'video link (subject)', specific programme detail, meetings with relevant programme staff and directors.

The aim is to seamlessly develop a relationship that deepens month by month. The relationship should be natural and completely authentic. You are motivated by the excitement of your programme and seeing each person engage more and more with you and your organisation. Enjoy these relationships. You certainly will meet some very interesting people.

At first the twelve month plan is a draft. However there will be plenty of opportunity to add to this plan every time you have direct contact with the donor as you learn more of their nuances. The best time to add to the twelve month plan is after completing the donor contact form (notes from your phone call or meeting). Continually develop the relationship chart and update it each time you learn something new.

As the year progresses the plan becomes less generic and more specific for that particular person. No two donor plans should be the same. They may look similar early in the relationship but as time progresses each plan will become very specific to each particular person.

If you are to be successful, you have to be in the driving seat a step ahead, following your plan month by month knowing where you want to go with the relationship.

principle _____ 32

The successful executive works through the dead months – January, August, September and December

It is a well known fact that it is extremely hard to secure major donor meetings in August and December. Perhaps in December it is slightly easier during the first week. After that it is difficult to get anyone's attention.

Usually you will experience the greatest success in booking meetings three weeks ahead. The reason for this is that next week your donor will know exactly how their week looks, the following week they pretty much know, it is the third week from now where they will see some gaps to possibly fit in a meeting. This is why September and January can also become barren months. If you only begin to make appointments in the first week of September, having had the break of August, then most of September becomes another 'dead' month for meetings.

It is possible to phone donors to arrange meetings in July up until the schools close. For private schools this is often the 12th or 13th July. It then becomes increasingly difficult to get hold of individuals and book appointments. However this may not apply if you have built the relationship to the point where you are a 'friend of the family', in which case there are more opportunities to engage within the holiday season. Or if the donor is single or child free as not everyone works to the school term calendar.

If the second half of July and August are difficult months to arrange meetings then likewise the month following, September, can also become a 'dead' month as you have not been able to arrange a meeting during August for September, likewise January. If you have not planned ahead then it is likely that both January and September will also become 'dead' months for meetings. In turn the two difficult months of the year can swiftly turn into four months, that is, one third of your year without appointments, unless you plan carefully.

The month of July particularly the first half of the month, is the month to look ahead, post August, to September and book as many meetings as possible, particularly for the first two weeks of September as they are the most difficult in which to secure meetings. If you have not booked meetings for the 1st – 14th September by the end of the school holidays in July it is unlikely that you will achieve this in August.

The same is true in the latter part of the year in the lead up to Christmas. This is because not many people like to arrange things or want to worry about 'one more thing' during the holiday season in the lead up to Christmas in December. Therefore book your January meetings in the second half of November to avoid meetings getting bumped into February.

The smart executive has the early September dates at the ready and books meeting dates in July. Similarly, in November the smart executive secures early January meeting dates.

How does this work practically? Have September dates at the ready when making your phone calls in July. If a person says to you: *'September! That is quite a way off...'* you can respond by saying something similar to *'Well it is good to get things in the diary now... I am away in August... I expect you are as well as it tends to be busy with family and holidays – how about 2nd September?'* This works really well and enables you to experience the success of having meetings all year round.

In summary, get appointments in August if you can as not everyone goes away but keep your eye closely on September and book up the first two weeks of the month during July. The same principle applies for December and January. Aim to book your meetings for the first two weeks of January by the end of November. It sounds obvious doesn't it but you would be amazed at how many executives leave it over the summer and then have a slow September start and leave it over Christmas and in turn experience a slow New Year start.

Once you have booked meetings at these times at least 6 weeks ahead, you can reassure yourself that you are all lined up for a strong autumn start. This has a knock on effect giving you a fast start to the prime months for major donor meetings in September, October and November. The same principle applies for early January giving you a strong start to the New Year.

principle _____ 33

The successful executive plans for a specific, high level £ 'ask' amount

One day a major gift executive was due to visit one of the major donors on her qualified caseload. She had been cultivating the relationship diligently each month for over six months and knew she had the right project match. The time had come to ask for the gift. She had prepared the proposal and was looking for an 'ask' of £12,000.

During our coaching session I asked her why this amount and how much was the total budget for the project in the proposal. The total project budget was £50,000. As we looked at the research on the person it became clear that this donor was capable of more than £12,000 and was very warm to the charity having given on a number of previous occasions, all of them at £12,000.

Now I can understand why she had her 'ask' set at £12,000. She was excited just to get another gift at the same level. However, as we discussed this she realised that actually, according to her background research, he could potentially give the whole sum. She changed her approach and asked him to give £50,000 to meet this need. It was a great success and he agreed to fund the project for the full £50,000.

A number of lessons can be learnt from this. Firstly it is important to ask the donor directly in person, always in a face-to-face situation. Never send the proposal ahead of your meeting. There are occasions when the prospective major donor insists on the proposal being sent, but by preference and as a general rule, do not agree to do this. It is far more effective for you to talk the proposal through with the person as you watch their reaction to everything you are saying.

Secondly, it is not advisable to put the 'ask' £ level in the proposal, rather insert the total project budget so you are free to decide the 'ask' £ amount in the face-to-face meeting. Sometimes the potential donor will also give you new information during the meeting such as *'By the way the maximum amount I can contribute to this is £10,000'* so you certainly don't want a proposal in your brief case ready to show him asking for a different amount. Or they may have a new objection that needs answering or may require more detailed questions about the budget.

Thirdly, not to pre-judge how much the donor will give, rather to ask high expectantly. Always ask for more £'s than you expect. Don't feel embarrassed to challenge your donor. At this stage of your relationship you should know each other well and trust is sufficiently built for you to be very honest and direct.

A major donor will soon let you know if it is too high. Remember they are on your side. They like your organisation. They want to help. The important part is that there is a strong relationship before the 'ask' is made. A minimum of 9 months of monthly touch points provides the basis for a good friendship. This is only a guideline as some donors are ready to give sooner in the relationship whilst others might need cultivation for over two years, only you are the judge as you are the only person who knows them well.

Generally, after a minimum of 9 months, your relationship will be strong enough for your potential donor to feel free to answer you honestly when you ask for a gift. More detail on how to make the 'ask' is in Book Two.

Bear in mind there should be a planned £ goal for every donor on your qualified caseload. This £ goal will be monitored and used for forecasting income for the year. If you want to be successful you will keep a private £ goal separately to challenge yourself and to challenge the donor to give at a higher level. Above everything, always remember that there is incredible joy in giving to something you believe in. Philanthropists want to make a difference in the world and are happy to be asked for high level £ amounts, you are helping each donor to achieve this.

principle _____ 34

The successful executive uses creative monthly touch points

You need a wide selection of different touch points to share with your donors. It is a good idea to keep a section on your server where you can file photos, links to videos and interesting personal stories on the key projects so they are easy to find. This may be centralised for the organisation, as other members of the fundraising team need this information as well, or just for the major gift team. This task is usually carried out and maintained by the administrator who is tasked to keep each project up-to-date with a wealth of interesting new material.

Contacting a donor is definitely a touch point but in some teams this is not counted as a touch point unless it is two-way and includes a response or follow-up. It would be very easy for an executive to be seen to be achieving a high number of touch points in a month by just sending out emails to all donors. If the donor doesn't reply and doesn't show any interest, the monthly report may show touch points as statistics but there is actually very little to demonstrate a deepening of the relationship. Worse still, they could be variations of the same email and therefore not personal at all.

This is not the ideal way for an executive to achieve quality touch points. On balance it is best practice to only count touch points that are two-way where the donor has replied or spoken to the executive. At least this shows some semblance of quality and development of the relationship.

Touch points should be very personal, tailored to the individual donor and as creative as your imagination can devise. Each touch point should either demonstrate the impact of their last donation or build the donor towards a specific 'ask' in the coming months based on the donor's passions and interests also including reference to their hobbies, personal interests and family.

Each touch point should prepare the way for the next month's touch point. For example, a thank you letter should close with a sentence such as 'I will arrange a meeting for you with our chief executive and call you to discuss the details' or 'Thank you again for your generous support. I will be in touch in the next few weeks to let you know how the project is progressing'.

There are many types of touch points and this is your opportunity to be as creative as you want to be as long as it is within the confines of what is suitable and appropriate for each person.

Sending information on a specific project to update the donor on how their gift is being used can take many forms. In some organisations it is sometimes difficult to acquire with only one report appearing every six months. In this case, the information may need to be dribbled to the donor gradually. For example, you could send a case study and photograph one month and more factual information the next month. The most important part is sending it in the way that best suits your donor and their preferences.

Some like a very detailed report of progress; others prefer short quick highlights of current progress on an email or text. Donors always like to hear your enthusiasm for the progress that is being made because of their generosity, so don't hold back.

Touch points with donors can include meetings or Skype calls with your chief executive, directors or programme staff. There are myriads of ways of taking short videos of staff or beneficiaries giving messages that are only a few seconds or one to two minutes long. These can be very encouraging for your donors.

The list of types of touch points is endless – photos, short stories, news stories that are relevant to your cause, articles, annual report, Christmas cards, Easter cards, birthday cards, postcards, all with a special message or story relevant for the individual's interest. Visits to the office can be arranged to meet a wide range of staff. If organising a visit, focus the visit around your donor's special interest as well as showing them (briefly) the length and breadth of your organisation. There is more detail on how to do this is in Book Two.

The use of very small lunches and dinners with perhaps just two or three donors present can bond your donor to key staff and perhaps to other donors with a similar interest.

There are also many different ways to say thank you for a gift – phone calls from programme staff and your chief executive, special thank you cards, framed photos, photo books demonstrating the difference your donor's gift has made. If you are creative then use that creativity to offer the donor an unforgettable experience. Each thank you should be designed for maximum meaningfulness for the donor.

Over time you may be able to offer them a place on an advisory board and bring them closer in to the central workings of your organisation. They may be interested in a specific aspect of your work and be able to offer skills, or even advice on the new strategy. Keep an open mind and facilitate the unfolding of a life-long relationship.

Occasionally it is necessary to send a letter to a donor. If this is the case then every letter should be topped and tailed by hand, preferably in blue ink with the use of a personal handwritten PS as this is often the most read part of a letter. In fact it is quite relational to handwrite the full letter on letterhead rather than typing. All envelopes should be handwritten with the use of a live first class stamp. Photos should also be printed out individually in a high quality resolution, held together by paperclip, to give a personal touch. Everything should be executed to a high standard to offer the best possible excellent service. This shows you care and will be appreciated.

Of course you won't always get it right. Learn from your donor's response to your communication and keep asking for their preferences. If they are not responding to the touch points then occasionally it can be chemistry. Perhaps you just don't click with the person and they aren't responding to you. If this is the case then involve someone else until the donor is responding.

You may need to pass the relationship over to someone with whom they do have great chemistry, for example, another team member or a director. Engage the director in the relationship to get it back on track and allow the director to front the relationship for you. You can still prepare the touch points and manage the plan by briefing the director. This can work well but does require careful communication as to who is doing what and when and a commitment of time and energy from the director.

Creative touch points, carefully chosen and executed are vital for the successful executive to ensure a meaningful relationship with each major donor.

principle _____ 35

The successful executive holds the correct relationship balance between personal and business

Your role is to build a healthy relationship with each donor through your personalised twelve month plan. However there is a fine balance between being 'over friendly' and losing the purpose of building the relationship towards philanthropy.

The relationship of benefactor and beneficiary organisation is different from business to business. In business, relationships are made with an understanding that it has an end business result. 'I am selling you a product or a service. I am connecting to you for this business purpose'. Conversations over dinner, lunch or during a round of golf have this understanding.

In philanthropy this line is blurred. I think this is partly because 'giving' by a philanthropist is not part of his or her business day, it is part of their leisure time. They give to make a difference. They are demonstrating a desire to care, to nourish, develop and to enhance the life of beneficiaries. He or she may well have business reasons for doing so and may organise their company to be philanthropic, however the mere act of giving goes way beyond business and can be quite deeply personal.

Therefore it can be hard sometimes for you as the executive to understand and manage that fine balance. You are building a friendly environment whereby the donor is enjoying your company and might even decide to involve his or her family to engage their children in this philanthropic experience. The donor may want to see your work first hand and is often happy to meet out of hours. I have known an executive join their philanthropist regularly on a long dog walk as it provided a suitable time to talk.

However, it is really important for the executive to get the right balance between 'friendship' and the need to 'steer' the relationship towards the end goal of securing funds for beneficiaries and doing it in such a way that it is enjoyable and rewarding for both parties. It can be quite a deep experience for the donor.

As part of this balance, it is the executive's responsibility to ensure that the relationship is built with the organisation rather than just themselves.

One of the ways to do this is to introduce your donor to other members of your team. You can include another team member on your visits or you can introduce team members when the donor visits your office. This can also include senior members of staff, your chief executive and directors. These relationships are crucial to the success of the relationship overall.

Be very clear on the goal and the planned strategy for your twelve month plan to keep driving the relationship gradually towards a beneficial result for both parties. It has to be more than just friendly meetings and phone calls. I have heard lots of executives say *'Well we are having lots of friendly conversations but whether it will result in a gift remains to be seen'*. This demonstrates a lack of understanding of what you are trying to achieve and you will not be successful if you only build a relationship made up of 'friendly conversations'. Make sure you are driving the relationship towards the 'ask' intentionally.

Ensure that the donor is enjoying the relationship but also growing in his or her understanding of your cause and its beneficiaries. Keep driving the relationship towards a deeper understanding of the work you do and the exciting results. Provide detail on vision and organisational strategy, project information and demonstrate the impact through video, stories and beneficiary successes.

Occasionally you may find yourself in some stagnant situations. To be successful you need to avoid some pitfalls. The first is to be too friendly without moving the relationship on towards giving. Another is asking for a gift too soon before trust has had time to build sufficiently. If you are experiencing some stagnation, it could be that you are not providing anything new to show or share and your donor is getting bored, withdraws and sees the relationship as time wasting.

At this point I would introduce a senior member of staff or trustee who has something new to share. If this doesn't work it could be that your prospective major donor truly is disinterested, in which case I would let them go. It is important in major gift work, that if someone is genuinely not interested, then donor choice prevails and you must graciously withdraw. However, try engaging them in every way you can before coming to this conclusion. It could be that your organisation is not top of their list at this moment in time, but this could change in the future.

It could also be your fault by not making enough frequent contact to engage the donor in your exciting work. This has to be a minimum of monthly. Perhaps you are not ensuring that the next touch point is agreed and in place before completing the phone call or visit. Or perhaps the chemistry is not working. As mentioned in Principle 34, use other team members or staff to front the relationship, who do have excellent chemistry. If in this predicament, definitely do not forge ahead with the relationship by yourself. This will undermine your success.

Every donor is different. Some take time to be won over. Others may have a different passion and interest to that being offered. Others may start the friendship but then drawback for time reasons. There are many variables. You need to persevere as some people take time to engage with you and your organisation, but you should also recognise when pursuing the relationship is a waste of their time and yours. You can do this without guilt remembering that it is likely you will only qualify one in three on to your caseload.

Picture yourself as a financial adviser offering some guidance to the philanthropist. Although your role is a personal relationship builder, the business part is to never lose sight of the goal – to help the philanthropist make a significant gift and see the difference their gift has made. There is a balance to be achieved in order for this to be fulfilling for them and rewarding for you.

principle 36

The successful executive reviews their progress monthly and includes a RAG status for each qualified individual

It is really important to keep setting goals and improving your work. When you first set up a major gift programme it is difficult to put goals in place. You are not sure what you need to be aiming for and you certainly don't have a history on which to base goals.

One way round this, during the first few months, is to monitor what you are doing and produce a report at the end of each month of activity. After a number of months you will begin to see a pattern emerging and this will help determine your future goals.

Monthly reporting on your team's activity is crucial for your leadership. This is especially true during the first two years when it takes longer to see income results. At first your director may not understand the need for this detail and may require gentle coaching on how important executive activity is in seeing the programme gain momentum. Your director initially may see it only as an income generating programme without realising all the benefits the programme can bring. He or she may only be interested in seeing bottom line income figures.

However, demonstrating the quality of donors on the database and the activity undertaken in the gradual building of the relationship with each donor will begin to inform leadership of the wide reaching impact of this programme. It is helpful to explain what you are doing and your methodology on a regular basis. A good platform for this is the monthly report.

Your team need a report to monitor their progress and your director can in turn see monthly progress of the number of donors contacted, their quality, cultivation and the number of key individuals who have been qualified. All this information builds confidence.

Reporting at month end can include numbers achieved for:

- Meetings with prospective major donors
- Meetings with qualified donors
- Phone calls
- Emails
- Letters/cards
- Missed calls (unsuccessful attempts to contact – this demonstrates how much time and how many attempts it takes to get through)
- Total number of contacts made (an active full-time executive should be achieving over 100 per month)
- Asks
- Leadership engaged
- Qualified donors on caseload
- Qualified donors contacted this month
- Newly qualified this month
- Prospective major donors (the executive's 'active' list)
- Prospective major donors contacted this month

If all donor contact is recorded on your database, it should be possible to generate contact statistics automatically at month end. However, experience shows that often these figures don't tally, therefore you might want to keep your own statistics manually to compare accuracy before relying on your database statistics.

As your programme develops keep adding more headlines to the monthly report. It is your shop window to leadership and all staff throughout the organisation as you endeavour to develop a culture of philanthropy where every staff member has some ownership of philanthropy. Sharing your statistics can help other staff to see how much work is involved.

It is helpful to add highlights and challenges for each team member. Leadership can see progress, understand the issues month by month and be instrumental in helping resolve the problems.

As the income grows you can add an income forecast for each

month of the year together with the actual £ achievement showing the year's month by month progression including gift aid and the number of gifts received over £10,000. It is also useful for leadership to see where that income has been allocated and which projects have been supported.

As the monthly report develops, start to add in a monthly target for meetings and phone calls and the actual numbers achieved against these targets. Also add in a RAG status, Red – Amber – Green for each qualified individual. Some teams even have a RAG status for prospective major donors. Define clearly what this means for your team. Here is an example:

RED: Missed contact for two months, not sure how to take the relationship forward

AMBER: Missed contact this month and some difficulty with the relationship

GREEN: Contacted this month, relationship strong and continuing to grow

In both the cases of Red and Amber the 'ask' is at risk and will need to be projected forward in the £ forecast. This may need to be reported up to senior leadership and may lead to a re-forecasting of income. It can show where cash flow could be at risk to meet end of year financial goals.

Giving a RAG status for each individual at the end of every month can also give a manager a clearer picture of what has been achieved, which is motivating for both parties and demonstrates the progression of all relationships.

Here is an example of a monthly report:

Key Relationship Team Monthly Report

Monthly Team Overview: (Manager to complete each month)

Highlights: (Executives and administrator complete each month)

Challenges: (Executives and administrator complete each month)

Financial Results

Year	Financial Year Budgeted Income		Financial Year Actual Income		= / -
	Monthly	Cumulative	Monthly	Cumulative	
Jan					
Feb					
March					
.....					
November					
December					
Total YTD					

Gift Income by Project

Allocation	Project 1	Project 2	Project 3	Project 4	Unrestricted	Total
Jan						
Feb						
March						
.....						
November						
December						
Total YTD						

Contact Statistics

Totals	Executive 1	Executive 2	Total
Calls – incoming *			
Calls – outgoing			
Calls – missed **			
Emails – incoming *			
Emails – outgoing			
Letters – incoming *			
Letters – outgoing			
Meetings			
No of times leaders engaged with donor			
Asks			
On site visits			

* Not every team records incoming statistics
** Missed call – attempted to get through but couldn't, including no answer, speaking to donor's PA or spouse

Annual Stats Tracker	Jan	Feb	....	Nov	Dec	Total
Calls – incoming						
Calls – outgoing						
Calls – missed						
Emails - incoming						
Emails – outgoing						
Letters - incoming						
Letters - outgoing						
Meetings						
No of times leaders engaged with donor						
Asks						
On site visits						

Executive Qualified Caseload and Prospective Major Donors			
At month End	Executive 1	Executive 2	Total
Qualified Caseload – total number			
Red			
Amber			
Green			
Newly qualified this month			
Unqualified this month			
Prospective major donors - number			
Red			
Amber			
Green			
New on 'active' list this month			
Deleted this month			
Transferred to Mid Value Programme			
Transferred to Legacy Programme			

Annual Tracker	Jan	Feb	Mar	.....	Oct	Nov	Dec	Total
Qualified Caseload – total								
Newly qualified this month								
Unqualified this month								
Prospective MD's – total								
New on 'active' this month								
Unqualified this month								

Total Donors Researched by Administrator						
	Donated £250+	Ranking List	Standing order or direct debit	Premier banking	Level 1 research complete	Level 2 research complete
Jan						
Feb						
.....						
Nov						
Dec						
TOTAL						

Notes:
- Prospect research is prioritised by: £250+ donation + signs of wealth; ranking list; standing order or direct debit; premier banking which are premier cheques received from a premier bank account and new direct debits set up using a premier bank account
- Level 1 takes only a few minutes to see if they are of interest to the major gift programme
- Level 2 involves more thorough research and referred to major gift executive

Over time I have increasingly wanted to find a more detailed method for demonstrating the depth of a relationship other than the use of Red, Amber and Green. I have developed a way of doing this using Levels of Engagement before a gift is given and Levels of Stewardship after a major gift is given. This is set out in more detail in Book Two.

principle 37

The successful executive prepares an annual review

The annual review is a culmination of all statistics from the year's monthly reports and includes some analysis of the findings. This is important for the team and demonstrates to leadership the progress of the team's work over the year including activity as well as finance. It may also include a narrative showing development of the programme year to year.

Leadership tend to look at finance primarily and therefore an annual review can help educate leadership regarding the extensive activity that is being achieved. It is this activity that will establish the longevity of the programme. It can take two to three years before the programme shows a high £ ratio return. The purpose of the monthly report is to show how well the team have done in developing the relationships even if income hasn't been delivered yet in the early financial years.

The first draft of the review is usually prepared by the administrator. Here are some suggestions of what to include in the annual review:

- Income total
- Income by months
- Current qualified caseload for executive; income raised this year compared to last year from that same group of donors
- % returning donors from previous financial year
- % new money
- % renewed that were lapsed (definition of lapsed is up to you – could be lapsed for 3 years)

- Number of gifts over £50k, £20 - £49k, £10k - £19k, under £10k (your own categories) and whether new gift or repeat gift
- Above as %'s
- Type of gift by % – regular giving, multi-year, one offs
- Trust gifts as % (personal trust giving)
- Breakdown for solicited and unsolicited gifts
- £'s pledged for next financial year by month (results taken from executive's relationship chart - £ forecast for next twelve months for every qualified donor)
- Prospective major donors on 'active' list contacted each month for year by executive
- Success rate for 'active' prospective major donors – number contacted, number converted
- Number of 'active' prospective major donors not yet qualified
- Number qualified (as at financial year end) and £ capacity
- Qualified dropped over the year (lack of continued interest)
- Lapsed big givers
- Locations of donors (on UK map - very interesting for directors to see)
- Number of couples, singles – male/female
- Interests by project type
- Qualified donors contacted each month for year by executive
- Meetings achieved each month for year by executive
- Phone calls each month for year by executive
- Missed calls each month for year by executive (important to monitor as executives spend a great deal of time phoning and not getting through!)
- Emails each month for year by executive
- Letters for each month for year by executive
- A summary of highlights and challenges

You will think of other areas that can be added in to your annual review. You will be amazed at how helpful this review is to look at trends and to provide the ground work for setting goals for the coming year and paving the way for further investment in the programme. To be successful, an annual review is essential.

principle   38

The successful executive audits their major donor work and allows it to pave the way for additional investment

As well as the annual review of compiled statistics, it is helpful to conduct an audit of your programme. Sometimes we can't see the 'wood for the trees'. The Cambridge Dictionary describes this phrase as '*to be unable to understand a situation clearly because you are too involved in it*'. If you are a director of fundraising, team leader or a major gift executive you may have developed your major gift programme recently or over a number of years with good intent, however, in spite of these best intentions, over time this may have been eroded due to many factors.

This could possibly be a change of staff, politics, reduced budget, a lack of evaluation or a slippery slope into bad habits, which all teams can do without constant reflection on performance. It is really essential to keep your standards high and to keep evaluating whether your programme is performing at full capacity.

This ideally should be carried out by an outside consultant who is experienced, impartial, unable to be lobbied and can benchmark against what others are achieving. This can give you a fresh look at what you are doing as a team and the individual performances. It can pick out the best, highlighting what is being performed well but conversely it can also help you to understand why one of the team is not performing well especially if the reason is unclear. There may be organisational blockages that need clearing.

It is also possible to appoint a member of staff to undertake this task. It can work if the staff member is relieved of all duties and is able to focus on the audit for as long as it takes, sometimes for over two months.

There are many areas to look at in a major gift programme audit with the purpose of ensuring your team are in tip top condition and performing at their best. It is simple enough to ask the questions – What do we want to achieve here? Is that being achieved? What is going well? What factors hinder this? What can be done to remove the blockage? All you need to do is ask these questions for each of the following topics:

- Values document for your major gift programme
- Wealth overlay of your database and how the results are used
- Ranking of donors and prospects
- Method for qualification of donors
- How major donors are engaged
- How £ goals are created for each major donor
- Formulation of plans for major donors
- How plans are currently tracked for each major donor
- How equipped current staff are for face-to-face meetings
- Is income at maximum capacity?
- How major donors are thanked/shown the difference they are making
- Awareness of the programme by senior staff and the board
- The case for support and projects available for major donors to fund
- Tracking and reporting income and expenditure
- Monthly reporting requirements
- Benchmarking analysis, how does giving from managed major donors compare to previous years, is it moving in an upward trend?
- Support for the programme, does the team feel supported? Where are the gaps?
- Programme tracking and management reporting, how is this achieved?
- Is the team sufficiently resourced with stories, reports and possible touch points?
- Process for working with regional staff
- Process for working with trustees and leadership
- Processes file – is it up-to-date and used as a reference?

The purpose of an audit is to strengthen your team, increase income and give you an opportunity to manage upwards to your directors and trustees. An audit can be a useful document for your leadership as they decide to invest further in the major gift programme. It will help to identify where your team are performing well and where improvement is needed and what costs that might entail.

The teams who are willing to improve and learn are the ones who will excel. An audit may cost a small fee but this is far outweighed by the increased income to your organisation and the improved relations with your directors and programme staff. I would advise having one every three years to make sure standards don't start to slide and to ensure you are on an upward trend and winning the race. If standards slip, you can guarantee your income will slip as well.

You may say 'as a consultant you are bound to say this'. Perhaps, but I get really frustrated when I see organisations let their major gift programme slide. It is so unnecessary and after it has started to slide, it becomes a much greater, more painful and far more expensive uphill task to get it back on track.

principle _____ 39

The successful executive plans three years ahead

When first planning a major gift programme, most people consider income as the most important goal. However it is almost impossible to predict income as little is known about prospective major donors at this early stage. However experience and best practice shows that income is related to two factors. One, the number of wealthy donors on your database and two, the number and effectiveness of staff employed to carry out the work of building relationships with donors.

Below is a chart that demonstrates how quickly a programme can build over a number of years:

Major gift executives	Income Year 1	Income Year 2	Income Year 3	Income Year 4
1	Up to £150k	£300k	£500k	£600k
2 added		£150k + £150k	£300k + £300k	£500k + £500k
2 added			£150k + £150k	£300k + £300k
Income*	**£150,000**	**£600,000**	**£1,400,000**	**£2,200,000**

*Assumption – there are at least 80 to 120 wealthy donors (given a gift, whatever size) identified in the wealth screening per executive

One executive can, typically, expect to secure £150,000 income in the first year. It is important to state that there is no guarantee for this and it is preferable for leadership to plan for no income in the first year. Income is different for each organisation and will depend on the number of wealthy donors and current givers on the database identified in the wealth screening and the completion of a successful organisational readiness study as described in Principle 2.

The above income figures are typical for the organisations I have worked with over many years. It can include income from engaged givers, who will give more when the relationship is approached in a more personal way. It can also include lapsed major donors who may not have been cared for since their last gift. In their first year, a new executive can show appreciation to lapsed givers, reignite their interest and, if matching their special interest to a project, often encourage them to give again.

£300,000 is a typical income figure for an executive in the second year and £500,000+ in an executive's third year provided they are fully supported by an administrator, prospect researcher and proposal and report writer and, to **emphasise** again here, there are sufficient numbers of prospective major donors on the database, at least 80 to 120 for each executive.

It is often good practice to recruit two major gift executives at the same time as they can train together, are at the same stage of development and will become a support to each other. This should seriously be considered for future years once leadership are confident that the major gift programme is growing. Those organisations that have been bold with their investment and recruitment have quickly accelerated their income by recruiting multiple executives at the same time.

In the planning, do not leave out the importance of employing an administrator at the same time as an executive. Support staff are crucial to allow freedom for the executive to carry out front line work with donors. Initially an administrator, sometimes referred to as the coordinator, can provide all three support roles of administration, prospect research and proposal and report writing.

It can be seen from the chart that the major gift programme is a highly worthwhile investment. The ratio between income and expenditure is very favourable. The following table shows the ratio between executives and support staff together with average staff costs:

Staffing	Year 1	Year 2	Year 3	Year 4
Total number Executives	1	3	5	5
Administrator responsible for admin, research, reports, proposals	1	1	1	1
Prospect Researcher		.5	1	1
Proposal and report writer		.5	1	1
*Staff Expenditure	£75,000	£200,000	£325,000	£325,000

* Assumed salaries at £50,000 (including national contributions and pension) for an executive and £25,000 for a support role, no allowance for inflation, no additional set up costs

As you can see from the diagram, the support staff are increased as more executives are employed.

When you start to compare income and expenditure in your three year plan you can begin to see how amazingly beneficial a major gift programme can be. Just bear in mind this is dependent on knowing that there are wealthy individuals on your database. The additional items to allow for the first year's budget are explained in more detail in Principle 7.

After the first twelve months, progress can be reviewed and a leadership decision made regarding future investment. A major gift programme is one of the most successful income generators for any organisation and, in some cases, can reach as much as the highest level income generators including legacies and institutional donors.

The major gift programme is tried and tested and will successfully build year on year as long as the key principles are followed.

Major Gifts Unwrapped – Book Two

49 Principles for the **Accomplished** Major Donor Fundraiser

This book includes the following:

- Characteristics of an effective major donor executive
- How to effectively engage your leadership
- Structuring the team
- How mid value and major gift programmes work together
- Use of capital campaigns
- Understanding a philanthropist's motivations
- Levels of engagement before the 'ask'
- Writing an effective 'ask' proposal
- How to 'ask' for a gift
- Using multi-year 'asks'
- Levels of stewardship after the 'ask'
- Donor visits to your office - 'Red Carpet Days'
- Importance of donor memories
- Common problems and how to overcome them

Printed in Great Britain
by Amazon